WHO RULES THE CHURCH?

WHO RULES THE CHURCH?

EXAMINING CONGREGATIONAL LEADERSHIP AND CHURCH GOVERNMENT

GERALD P. COWEN

BROADMAN
&HOLMAN
PUBLISHERS

NASHVILLE, TENNESSEE

Published by Broadman & Holman Publishers
Nashville, Tennessee

Dewey Decimal Classification: 253
Subject Heading: PASTORAL WORK \ CHURCH
ADMINISTRATION \ LEADERSHIP

Biblical text is identified by the following acronyms: KJV, King James
Version. NASB, the New American Standard Bible, © the Lockman
Foundation, 1960, 1962, 1963, 1968, 1971, 1972, 1973, 1975, 1977;
used by permission. NEB, The New English Bible, © The Delegates of
the Oxford University Press and the Syndics of the Cambridge
University Press, 1961, 1970, reprinted by permission. NIV, The Holy
Bible, New International Version, copyright © 1973, 1978, 1984 by
International Bible Society. NKJV, New King James Version, copyright ©
1979, 1980, 1982, Thomas Nelson, Inc., Publishers.

4 5 6 7 8 9 10 08 07 06 05 04

Contents

115435

Foreword

Jerry Vines
Pastor, First Baptist Church
Jacksonville, Florida

Are you looking for a book that gives a thorough study of the whole pastor-elder issue? Well, you now have such a book in your hands! Those of us who have known and appreciated Dr. Gerald Cowen for many years expect anything from him to be thoroughly researched and well done. The book you hold in your hands is exactly that kind of book. We would also expect it to be a very helpful study of the Greek text. The book you hold in your hands is certainly that.

Dr. Cowen gives a very good study of the whole New Testament teaching on the subject of pastor-elder. Drawing from his extensive knowledge of and skill in the Greek language, he shows us exactly how all the terms related to pastor-elder are used.

The first chapter is well worth the price of the book. I would encourage you to read this chapter carefully and follow his analysis. He proves to my satisfaction that the terms *pastor, elder,* and *bishop* are used interchangeably to refer to the same office. Also, he gives a very good study of the meaning of the word *deacon*.

The role and authority of the pastor-elder are thoroughly discussed from a biblical and linguistic standpoint.

These chapters will be very helpful for those called to be pastors and also for churches as they seek to find a pastor to lead their congregations.

The discussions relative to qualifications for the office are biblical and extremely current in today's atmosphere. All pastors and all congregations seeking a pastor should give careful, prayerful thought to these qualifications. The relationship of a pastor-elder and his deacons can be absolutely vital to the successful fulfillment of a local church's ministry. Having been a pastor now for over forty years, I can say without fear of contradiction that no pastor can be as effective as he would like to be and should be unless he has a group of spiritual-minded, godly men to assist him. Looking back over the years of my ministry, my strongest supporters and greatest helpers have been godly, Jesus-loving deacons.

The second chapter of the book may be the best one. In a day when we are hearing very little about the importance of a called ministry, Dr. Cowen establishes beyond question that the role of the pastor is one to which a man must be called by God.

I commend this good book to you. I commend this faithful biblical and Greek scholar to you. He has given us a book that will be a constant source of reference.

Jerry Vines
Pastor, First Baptist Church
Jacksonville, Florida

Introduction

There is, at this point in time, a great deal of confusion and debate over who should lead the church and how they should do it. George Barna reports the results of a recent survey which says that fewer than one in eight senior pastors in the United States identify themselves as leaders and less than 10 percent can articulate God's vision for the ministry of their church.[1] There are a number of models of church leadership that are being touted by different groups. Some of them include the CEO model, where leadership descends from one person. Another model, elder rule, is being encouraged by some.[2] Under this model a small group of elders, either chosen by the congregation or by a self-perpetuating board, controls the church. Another model is a type of congregational rule that emphasizes lay leadership. Under this model the pastor becomes a servant of the church but not the leader. He functions as a sort of chaplain to the congregation.

Barna supports this model when he says, "Too many churches expect to find leadership from a position instead of from someone who feels called to lead." He adds that God has brought us leaders—they are in the pews.[3] It is said under this view that turning leadership over to the lay people can free the pastor for more ministry. But is that the biblical model?

There are some who maintain that the New Testament does not favor any particular view of church organization. The well-known New Testament scholar G. E. Ladd says in his work *A Theology of the New Testament*: "It appears likely that there was no normative pattern of church government in the apostolic age, and that the organizational structure of the church is no essential element in the theology of the church."[4] Some might agree with Ladd that since the New Testament does not give us an exact blueprint on these matters, churches are free to organize as they see fit. More likely, however, this is not the case.

Robert Saucy is correct when he observes that what one sees in the New Testament is a growing and developing body. Therefore, it is "difficult to get a unified view of what a mature, fully developed church (if there is such) should be."[5] In the beginning of the church, leadership was located in the apostles, and elders were not mentioned. Later, elders were mentioned in the Jerusalem church (Acts 11:30) and were appointed in other churches (Acts 14:22). Later in their ministry, two of the apostles, Peter and John, called themselves "elders" (2 John 1; 3 John 1; 1 Pet. 5:1). Deacons were elected to serve under the apostles and elders (Acts 6). As the church began to multiply and spread to cities outside of Israel, an organizational structure began to appear. No organizational chart is given anywhere in Scripture, but there are vignettes or cameos of the church in action that show us some of its basic organizational principles.

The thesis of this work is this: there is a New Testament model, and it is the congregational model. Authority is given by the Lord to the congregation itself. However, the pastor is a God-called, God-ordained person who not only serves and takes care of the congregation but is the leader of the church. This model could be called Pastoral Leadership-Congregational Rule.

This work will attempt to define what a pastor or elder is, what his job description is, and what the limits of his authority are. A number of related questions will also be discussed because of their bearing on the main thesis of this book. Among these are: Must a pastor be called to this ministry? How many pastor-elders should a church have? What qualifications must a pastor have?

Defining a Pastor-Elder

There are many differing views in the world today about the role of pastors, elders, and other church officials. To begin this study, these terms need to be clearly defined in their New Testament context. What is a pastor? What is an elder? Are pastors and elders the same? Are they different offices? What does the New Testament say?

Pastor

The most popular term today for the spiritual leader of a church is *pastor*. However, in the New Testament the term is most often used to refer to a shepherd. It is used eighteen times, fifteen of which are in the Gospels. Jesus preaches a sermon in John 10 that describes what a good shepherd is like. He Himself is the great example, the Good Shepherd. Peter, who heard this discourse, calls Jesus "the Shepherd and Bishop of your souls" (1 Pet. 2:25 KJV). The author of Hebrews refers to Jesus as that "great Shepherd of the sheep" (Heb. 13:20 NIV).

The only reference to the office of pastor *(poimen)* is in Ephesians 4:11. It is found in a list of the spiritual gifts given to the church. Paul says, "He Himself gave some to be apostles, some prophets, some evangelists, and some pastors and teachers" (NKJV). Ephesians 4 seems to indicate that the gift of pastor is indeed inseparable from the gift of teacher. Pastor and teacher are one office, not two. In other words a pastor is a pastor-teacher. Although he may have other gifts, the pastor must be a teacher because this is an essential part of the pastor's ministry.

In addition, the verb form of shepherd (poimaino) is used eleven times. It is used in Jesus' admonition to Peter in John 21:16. Three times Jesus asks Peter, "Do you love me?" The second time Peter replies, "You know that I love you." Jesus then instructs Peter, "Feed (poimaino) my sheep" (NIV). The first and third times Jesus asks the question of Peter, his instruction to "feed my lambs" and "feed my sheep" uses the word baske, which literally means "to feed." Poimaino, on the other hand, means to do more than "feed" them. It means "to tend to them" or to "shepherd the sheep."

Acts 20:28 also uses the verb form pastor. Speaking to the elders of the church in Ephesus, Paul instructs them to "take heed" first to themselves and then to the "flock among which the Holy Spirit has made you overseers" (episcopoi or bishops, NIV). He explains what this means by adding the words "to shepherd [pastor] the church of God which He purchased with His own blood." It is an interesting sidelight that Luke avoids saying the pastor's job is to be "over" the flock, and says instead that the pastor works "among" the flock.

First Corinthians 9:7 also speaks of a shepherd tending a flock. If the shepherd takes care of the flock, then he should also make his living financially from that which the flock produces. It is clear from the context that Paul is not using this illustration to refer to literal sheep only. He is illustrating the fact that a shepherd (pastor) has the right to be paid by the flock. He asks, "Who ever goes to war at his own expense?" (NKJV). He answers his own question in verse 14: "Even so the Lord has commanded that those who preach the gospel should live from the gospel" (NKJV).

Peter admonishes the elders from Pontus, Galatia, Cappadocia, Asia, and Bithynia to "shepherd [pastor] the flock of God which is among you, serving as overseers [bishops]" (1 Pet. 5:1–4). In giving this instruction to pastor or shepherd the flock, Peter gives four guidelines. As they oversee the flock, they are (1) not to use "compulsion"; (2) not to serve for the sake of "dishonest gain"; (3) not to "Lord it over" those entrusted to their care; and (4) to be examples to the flock.

In contrast to true shepherds, the false teachers described by Jude feed (pastor) only themselves. They are like clouds without water. They show a lot of promise but leave the flock without spiritual benefit (v. 12).

Other uses of the word *poimaino* refer to Jesus, the Great Shepherd. He is the great example for all other shepherds to follow. It was predicted that out of Bethlehem would come a "ruler who will shepherd my people Israel" (Matt. 2:6). It is interesting that John predicts that the "Lamb who is in the midst of the throne will shepherd [pastor] them and lead them to living fountains of water" (Rev. 7:17 NKJV). It is clear that part of pastoring is leading.

In three places the word *poimaino* means "to rule." It refers to Jesus, who will "rule all nations with a rod of iron" (Rev. 12:5 NKJV). When Jesus returns to judge the nations, He will "strike the nations," and "He Himself will rule them with a rod of iron" (Rev. 19:15 NKJV). Finally, those who have been faithful, those who have overcome, will receive "power over the nations" and will "rule" with Him (Rev. 2:27).

Bishop

While looking at the Greek words referring to the office of pastor and the work of pastoring the flock, another term appears in two of the passages. Jesus is called the "Shepherd and Bishop [overseer] of your souls" (1 Pet. 2:25 KJV). The terms are used as synonyms. In this passage a shepherd is an overseer of the sheep. The two terms also seem to refer to the same office in Acts 20:28. Addressing the elders from Ephesus, Paul says that the Holy Spirit made them "overseers" (bishops, *episkopoi)*, and their job is to "shepherd" or "pastor" the church. When Paul writes to the Philippian church, he addresses the "saints," with the "bishops and deacons" (Phil. 1:1 KJV). It is clear in this case that Paul is speaking of offices in the church, not just functions. They are positions of leadership in the church.

The office is mentioned again in 1 Timothy. Paul says that the "position [office] of a bishop" is a good work. He then discusses the qualifications necessary for this position (1 Tim. 3:2–7). The qualifications for bishop are discussed again in Titus 1:6–9. In Titus, Paul seems to equate the office of bishop and elder again. He talks about appointing "elders in every city," and then he begins a discussion of the qualifications (Titus 1:5–6). In the middle of the discussion, he changes the title of the same office to "bishop" (1:7).

The verb form *episkopountas* is used in Hebrews 12:15. The "bishop" is to look "carefully" (oversee) lest anyone come short of salvation or lest any fall into spiritual errors such as "bitterness" (vv. 15–17). The same form of the word is found in 1 Peter 5:1–2. The "elders" are told to "shepherd the flock of God . . . serving as overseers." The duties of a bishop or overseer are (1) to watch over the spiritual welfare of those under his charge, and (2) to see that things done by others are done correctly.

Elder

The term *elder* is by far the most common term used in the New Testament to denote an officer in a local church. The term *presbuteros* is used sixty-six times in the New Testament. The term can be used of age to refer to one who is a senior in rank, such as in Acts 2:17. Here it is used in contrast to the young men: "Your old men shall dream dreams" (NKJV). First Timothy 5:1 also has this meaning: "Do not rebuke an older man, but exhort *him* as a father."

This use of the term is carried over from the Old Testament where it was used to refer to the older men who helped govern in the Jewish community. Many of the uses of *elder* in the New Testament refer to the Jewish elders. In Matthew 16:21 some members of the great council, the Sanhedrin, were called "elders." Thayer says, "In early times, the rulers of the people, judges, etc., were selected from the elderly men."[1]

There are also twelve occurrences of the term *elder* in Revelation. All of these references refer to the twenty-four elders who are seated around the throne of God (e.g., Rev. 4:4). They make up what might be called the heavenly Sanhedrin.

At least eighteen times the term *elder* is used to refer to an officer in the local church. The first mention is in Acts 11:30. Barnabas and Saul took the offering for the poor from Antioch and brought it to the "elders" in Jerusalem. Several times the "elders" are mentioned in connection with the Jerusalem Conference. In order to settle the dispute with the Judaizers, who were saying, "Unless you are circumcised according to the custom of Moses, you cannot be saved," the church at Antioch sent a delegation with Paul and Barnabas to Jerusalem "to the apostles and elders" (Acts 15:1–2 NKJV). They were received by the church, including "the apostles and elders" (15:4 NKJV), and then the leaders, the "apostles and elders came together to consider this matter" (15:6). When a decision was reached, the matter was brought before the whole church with the apostles and elders and approved (15:22). A letter was then composed to be sent out to other churches concerning this matter. It was sent from the "apostles, the elders, and the brethren" (15:23) to the brethren in Antioch, Syria, and Cilicia. The decree from the "apostles and elders at Jerusalem" is also mentioned in Acts 16:4, when Paul delivered it to Lystra. It is interesting to note that in the last reference to the Jerusalem "elders," the apostles are not mentioned as being present. In this case Paul went to Jerusalem after his third missionary journey. He was welcomed by the brethren and the next day had a meeting with James, and "all the elders were present" (21:18 NKJV). This probably means that in the years between A.D. 49 and A.D. 57 the apostles had become engaged in spreading the gospel elsewhere.

In addition to the elders of the Jerusalem church, Luke says that Paul and Barnabas "appointed elders in every church." They started this practice on their first missionary journey (Acts 14:23). They did so "praying and with fasting." They did not leave any church leaderless, but they chose leaders and "commended them to the Lord." So from the beginning, churches had a certain amount of organization.

The church in Ephesus also had elders. How and when they were selected is not described in Acts. Luke mentions, however, that Paul called for them to meet him in Miletus as he was returning to Jerusalem at the end of his third missionary journey (Acts 20:17–37). There are a number of important facts that may be learned about elders in this passage, but only one will be cited at this point. In verse 28 Paul instructs the elders to "take heed . . . to all the flock among which the Holy Spirit has made you overseers." The word *overseer* is *episkopos* or *bishop*. In this passage the title *elder* is again used interchangeably with *bishop*.

Paul gave instructions to Titus that he was to "set in order the things that are lacking" (Titus 1:5 NKJV). Part of this setting things in order was to "appoint elders in every city" in Crete. Paul then gave Titus the qualifications for being appointed an elder.

It is interesting that Paul gives Timothy a similar list of qualifications for choosing "bishops." He does not mention bishops again in 1 Timothy, but later in the epistle he does give the church instructions about how to treat elders. First, Paul asks that elders who "rule well be counted worthy of double honor" (1 Tim. 5:17 NKJV). The word *rule* refers to leadership. The word *honor* may refer to remuneration.

The second instruction concerning elders comes right after the first one. It is in regard to accusations of wrongdoing against an elder. (1) Do not receive the accusation unless there are at least two or three witnesses (v. 19); however, (2) if the elder is found to be guilty, "rebuke" him publicly, "in the presence of all" (v. 20).

Elders are also mentioned several times in the General Epistles. James says in his epistle that a believer who is sick has the right to call for the elders of the church to pray over him (James 5:14). The Apostle John refers to himself as an elder in his introduction of himself in both 2 John 1 and in 3 John 1.

Peter gives instructions to the elders of the churches in Pontus, Galatia, Cappadocia, Asia, and Bithynia (1 Pet. 1:1; 5:1–3). He commands them to "shepherd the flock of God . . . serving as overseers [bishops]." It has been observed previously that "to shepherd" means "to pastor" the church. Peter then gives them some guidance on how to pastor the churches: "not by compulsion . . . but being examples to the flock" (5:2–3 NKJV). In this passage Peter approaches the elders on common ground. He writes that he himself, although an apostle, is also an elder, and in the same passage he reminds them that Jesus is the Chief Shepherd (Pastor) of the church (5:1, 4).

In addition to giving instructions to the elders, Peter gives instructions to the church concerning its attitude toward elders. He tells the younger people to "be sub-missive to your elders" (5:5). One might contend that this passage refers only to those who are old in age as being worthy of this kind of respect. However, the context of the preceding verses shows clearly that Peter is talking about the office of elder, and so it is best to apply it to those who hold this office, regardless of their chronological age. The elders are appointed to their office because they have the necessary spiritual qualifications. They have been called of God to serve, and they have been ordained by the church. On this basis they are worthy of respect due to the office itself.

The Relationship of Pastor, Bishop, and Elder

It has been observed in my previous discussion that there is a connection between these three terms. At least three passages indicate that these terms refer to the same office. (1) Paul addresses the elders from Ephesus (Acts 20:17) and tells them that the Holy Spirit has made them overseers (bishops) of the flock, and they are to shepherd (pastor) the church (v. 28). (2) There is a similar admonition in 1 Peter. Peter addresses the elders (5:1) and then directs them to "shepherd" (pastor) "the flock of God" . . . "serving as overseers" (bishops) of the church (5:2). (3) In Paul's letter to Titus, Paul gives qualifications for the office of elder (1:3). Yet in the middle of the list of qualifications for "elders," Paul says, "For a bishop must be blameless" (1:6 NKJV). Speaking of the same office, Paul uses two different titles.

(4) One other fact should be noted. There is no church in the New Testament that has more than two permanent offices in its leadership structure. Philippians 1:1 addresses the bishops and deacons of that church. The Jerusalem church had elders and chose the first deacons (Acts 6:1–7). Paul gives the qualifications for bishops and deacons in 1 Timothy 3.

Two conclusions can be drawn from this evidence. First, *pastor, elder,* and *bishop* all refer to the same office. The terms are used interchangeably. Although the term *pastor* is commonly used today as the title for the spiritual overseer of a congregation, it was probably not intended in Scripture to be a title but to be descriptive of what an elder does. Robbins is correct when he says that it is a "metaphoric description of one who cares for and leads a flock of God's sheep."[2] *Bishop* (overseer) also describes the nature of the work of the pastor-elder. It definitely does not describe a separate hierarchical office such as is found in some groups today. The most common term in the New Testament for this office is *elder*. This was the preferred title in New Testament times, but the titles *pastor* and *bishop* are also used for the same office. Second, there are two—and only two—permanent offices in the church:

pastor-elder-bishop and deacon. No qualifications are given for any other office.

Lightfoot summed up the issue over a century ago, but it needs to be said again: "It is a fact now generally recognized by theologians of all shades of opinion, that in the language of the New Testament the same office in the Church is called indifferently 'bishop' (*episkopos*) and 'elder,' or 'presbyter' (*presbuteros*)."[3]

Bishops were pastor-elders of one church, and there is no hint in the New Testament that they had any authority over any other churches except the one they pastored. How many elders should a New Testament church have? The New Testament does not tell us specifically how many pastor-elders a church should have. There are no commands on that subject. It is true that whenever the term *elder* or *bishop* is used in the New Testament it is used in the plural, which would mean that the general practice of the churches in New Testament times was to have at least two elders. Acts 14:23 reports that Paul and Barnabas "ordained elders in every church." In Philippians 1:1 the apostles greet the "bishops and deacons." The Jerusalem church had "elders" (Acts 15:4ff.; 16:4; 21:18). Even though there is no explicit instruction on how to decide how many elders a church should have, it is argued by some that to be biblical, a church must have multiple elders.

Why is it then that in the present day the vast majority of churches have only one elder (pastor)? Are churches today simply not following Scripture in their practice? Perhaps. However, the issue is not quite that simple. While it may be agreed that the New Testament talks about multiple elders, a closer look must be taken at the situation in the New Testament churches, and then one must compare the first-century context with the present situation.

Although the church in Jerusalem had multiple elders, no number is given, nor is it described how they were chosen and deployed. Acts 4:4 does say that the number of the male *(andron)* believers was about five thousand.[4] This means that the Jerusalem church numbered possibly as many as twenty thousand persons (including women and children). How then did they assemble for worship? Scripture says they met "publicly and from house to house" (Acts 2:46; 20:20). They did not have church buildings at that time, so it is likely that they met in homes around the city. Each of these "home churches" would need a pastor-elder to lead the group. They could have had more than one, but no one knows. The key point is that they considered themselves to be one church—the church which is at Jerusalem (see Acts 15). They were one church with many house congregations and many elders.

Compare that to the modern church. Believers are divided into many denominations with many different congregations. These often have little or no fellowship with each other. Even churches of the same denomination in the same city do not consider themselves to be part of a larger group. There is no such thing today as a physical entity or group called the church in Dallas or the church in Atlanta. Each local group considers itself to be totally separate as far as pastoral leadership is concerned. This is in stark contrast with the unity the church enjoyed in the first century. So comparing the number of elders may be somewhat misleading. The argument may not apply at all to our present situation. Because the church is now so divided, there is little or no possibility of restoring it to its original unity.

Regardless of the number of elders there were in each city or local church, one man of God always seems to have been the pastor. The great example of this kind of leadership is found in the Jerusalem church itself. When the church met for the Jerusalem Conference (Acts 15), one man presided over the meeting and led them to a decision. That man was James, the brother of Jesus. Though there were many elders, there was only one leader. The model seems to have been that there were pastor-elders over each house congregation but only one leader. One might call James the senior pastor of the Jerusalem church.

The letters to the seven churches in the Book of Revelation are illustrations of this very thing (chs. 2–3). Each of the letters is addressed to the "angel" of the church. There are many interpretations as to the identity of these "messengers," and a firm conclusion cannot be reached. However, the vast majority of Bible commentators conclude that these are addressed to the "pastor" of the church. One could interpret the word *angel* or *messenger* as an angelic being attached to each church.[5] But what sense would it make for the letter to be given from the Lord to John to an angel to the church. It is much more logical that the message was communicated to the pastor, who then read it to the church. These churches also may have had multiple elders, but there was one who was "the pastor" of the church.

2

The Call of a Pastor-Elder

Many established old-line Protestant denominations are having a difficult time getting young people in their churches to take interest in devoting their lives to pastoral ministry. As a result these churches will be facing a serious shortage of pastors in the near future. Because of the problem, churches are being instructed in how to recruit young people for the ministry (see chart below). The Fund for Theological Education staff, the Lilly Endowment officers, and many seminary and church officials met recently to come up with a plan. Their model calls "lay leaders within a congregation to invite a talented young person for a trial year in seminary funded by a partnership of seminary, congregation and the FTE."[1]

Ordained Clergy Under 35[2]

American Baptist	5.8%
Disciples of Christ	3.7%
Episcopal Church	3.9%
ELCA	6.1%
PSUSA	7.0%
United Church of Christ	4.0%
United Methodist	6.7%

This approach may be a good attempt at solving the problem from a pragmatic point of view. However, from a biblical perspective it holds little, if any, promise for the future. The traditional view is that to become a minister (pastor) one must be "called" by God. If this view is correct, then such a high calling cannot be initiated from the human side. Let us look at the biblical evidence.

Scriptural Precedents

The precedent for this view began with the Old Testament prophets. God designated them with a special calling. First, there was the prophet Isaiah, who describes his dramatic call and surrender to be God's prophet: "Also I heard the voice of the Lord, saying: 'Whom shall I send, and who will go for Us?' Then I said, 'Here am I! Send me'" (Isa. 6:8–9a).

Jeremiah begins his book of prophecy with an account of his call from God (Jer. 1:4–5). He says, "Then the word of the Lord came to me, saying: 'Before I formed you in the womb I knew you; before you were born I sanctified you; I ordained you a prophet to the nations.'" Jeremiah also records his struggle against that call and his inability to escape it. He uses excuses such as, "I am a youth," but to no avail (Jer. 1:6). He tries to quit at one point because of the mocking he endures, but he cannot because God's word was in his heart "like a burning fire" (Jer. 20:8–9).

Ezekiel's call was similar to those of Isaiah and Jeremiah. The likeness of the glory of the Lord appeared to him, and God spoke to him (Ezek. 1:28–2:2). The Spirit entered into him and the Lord said to him, "Son of man, I am sending you to the children of Israel, to a rebellious nation that has rebelled against Me; . . . You shall speak My words to them" (Ezek. 2:3, 7a).

Hosea's experience was somewhat different from those mentioned so far. Scripture says the "word of the Lord came to Hosea" and "the Lord began to speak by Hosea" (Hos. 1:1–2). In the same manner the "word of the Lord came to Joel" whereby he was instructed to prophesy to his people (Joel 1:1ff.). In both cases God began to speak to these men, giving them a message and charging them to deliver it in His name.

Perhaps the most striking account of God's call to a prophet in the Old Testament is that of Amos. He describes his call as God "taking him" from his previous occupation as a sheepherder and a cultivator of sycamore fruit. Amos clearly says it was not his idea to choose such an office, but he was obedient to God's call.

> Then Amos replied to Amaziah, "I was no prophet, nor was I the son of a Prophet; but was a sheepherder and a tender of sycamore fruit. But the Lord took me as I followed the flock and the Lord said to me, 'Go prophesy to My people Israel'" (Amos 7:14–15).

Other accounts include the call of Jonah (1:1–2), which says, "Now the word of the Lord came to Jonah the son of Amittai, saying, 'Arise, go to Ninevah, that great city, and cry out against it.'" Nahum (1:1), Habakkuk (1:1), and Malachi (1:1) all describe their motivation to prophesy as a "burden" the Lord gave them and from which they could not escape. In every case it was God who initiated the action. He gave them a message and told them to speak. Some like Jonah tried to escape the call of God, but they were not able to avoid it.

In addition to the writing prophets, the call of Samuel is recorded in 1 Samuel 3. Three times it is said that God called Samuel to be His spokesman. In 1 Kings 17:1–3 the

Lord calls Elijah to deliver His message to Israel. Scripture says that "he went and did according to the word of the Lord" (17:5). Someone may say, "But these are Old Testament examples and things were different then. Maybe God does not work in the same way anymore." What is the New Testament evidence? Are there New Testament precedents as well? In the New Testament the call of the apostles by Jesus Himself is clearly set forth. Several of these accounts involving Jesus' disciples are recorded in the Gospels.

First, Jesus called the four fishermen: Peter, Andrew, James, and John. The importance of their call is underscored by the fact that the accounts are recorded in three separate Gospels (Matt. 4:18ff; Mark 1:16–20; and Luke 5:1–11). Mark gives the short version, which says that Jesus walked by the Sea of Galilee one day, saw Peter and Andrew fishing, and instructed them to follow Him. He went a little farther and saw James and John and "immediately He called them." All the accounts record them immediately leaving their business to follow Him. This seems a bit strange that they would follow a stranger so readily, if he were indeed a stranger. Upon reflection it becomes clear that this was not the first time they had met Him—otherwise they would not have been qualified to be apostles. When Peter proposed a replacement for Judas in Acts 1:21–23, the qualification was someone who had been with them from the time of John's baptism. This is presumably Jesus' baptism by John, which marked the beginning of Jesus' ministry.

The call of Levi (Matthew) is recorded by both Mark and Luke. Mark 2:14 says as Jesus "passed by, He saw Levi the son of Alphaeus sitting at the tax office. And He said to him, 'Follow Me.'" He immediately left his position at the tax office and followed Jesus.

The call of the other apostles is described in Mark 3:13. Jesus went up on the mountain and "called to Him those He Himself wanted." When they had come to Him, He "appointed twelve that they might be with Him and that He might send them out to preach." In verses 10–19 the complete list of the twelve is given (see also Luke 5:12–16 and Matt. 10:1–4). In every case the call came from the Lord. None of the twelve decided on his own to become an apostle.

In addition to the twelve, there was the call of the Apostle Paul. In the introduction to Romans, Paul describes his call to preach. He says he is "called to be an apostle separated to the gospel of God" (Rom. 1:1). In Galatians 1:1 he explains that his apostleship is "not from men nor through man, but through Jesus Christ and God the Father." In five other epistles he introduces himself as one who is an apostle "by the will of God" (1 Cor. 1:1; 2 Cor. 2:1; Eph. 1:1; Col. 1:1; and 2 Tim. 1:1). In 1 Timothy 1:1 and Titus 1:3, Paul declares that he is an apostle by the "commandment of God." It is very obvious that Paul's call from God was extremely important to him. His authority as an apostle was based on the fact that the message he was preaching, he was preaching according to the will of God. It was not his choice. He speaks of the saving ministry of Christ (1 Tim. 2:5–7) and explains that he was "appointed a preacher and an apostle" to proclaim that message. Paul gave a brief testimony to the Galatians which included his call. He was zealous for Judaism in his early life, but as he says, "When it pleased God, who separated me from my mother's womb and called me through His grace, to reveal His Son in me, that I might preach

Him among the Gentiles," he did not confer with any human authorities (1:15–16). His call was from God, and his message was from God. His only decision was whether to obey the call of God.

In addition to Paul's original call to preach, he received another call, along with Barnabas, to take the gospel to the Gentiles. This call is explained in a little more detail. (1) It happened as they were ministering and fasting at Antioch (Acts 13:2). (2) The Holy Spirit initiated the call. It is not clear whether only Paul and Barnabas received the message or others in the church received the same message from God. (3) They were instructed to "separate" or "consecrate" them for a special purpose. (4) The church then was called to fast and pray over this matter. This was apparently for the purpose of verifying the will of God in the call of these men. (5) When they had completed their prayer and were satisfied with their findings, the church "laid hands on them" and then sent them on their way. This demonstrated that the church concurred with their call, that it was from God, and that they went forth with the support and blessing of the Antioch church.

Interpretations of the Precedents

While the biblical evidence is clear that prophets in the Old Testament were called and that New Testament apostles and even some missionaries were called, some still argue that the New Testament does not clearly say that a pastor must be called. Many precedents have been cited, but precedents are not commands or even directions. Some argue that a person can decide to become a pastor if he has a "desire" to do so and if he has the gifts necessary for the office. No special call of God is necessary. This view is based on 1 Timothy 3:1: "If a man desires the position of a bishop, he desires a good work." Those who take this position argue that since the New Testament does not stipulate exactly how the process is to work, each person is free to make his own decision.

The Wisdom View

Gary Friesen, for example, argues that these are only three New Testament examples of a call to a "specific function of office."[3] These, he says, are the exception rather than the rule. His reasons are these: (1) In each case the means of communication was some form of supernatural revelation. (2) These vocational calls were "issued only to certain individuals at certain times."[4] His conclusion is that Acts makes clear that the Holy Spirit was closely superintending the early church's growth. However, God intervenes at decisive moments and the rest of the time He leaves saints to carry on by wisely interpreting and applying the moral will of God as it is revealed in Scripture. (3) The special call of God was always unsought and unexpected, and there are no directions to Christians to seek out such a call. (4) Finally, Friesen argues that calling in the vocational sense occupies a minor place in Scripture. While he admits God could still make such choices and reveal them as He did in the past, Scripture indicates that God did not normally lead that way in Bible times.[5]

In answer to Friesen, it is true that there are not many accounts of calling to a special office in the New Testament; however, there are some cases recorded. How many does it take for it to be true? The three cases he mentions are Paul's call to be an apostle (Acts 26:14–20), Barnabas and Paul's call to be missionaries (Acts 13:2), and Paul and his associates' call to evangelize Macedonia

(Acts 16:9–10). His conclusion is that all of the cases were the result of supernatural or special revelation. However, there is no evidence that the call of Paul and Barnabas to mission work was that sort of call. Acts says that the Holy Spirit told them to set apart Paul and Barnabas for this work. There is no indication that this was some kind of audible instruction. If it were, why was it necessary for the whole church to fast and pray to confirm the validity of this call? It was more likely an inner leading of the Holy Spirit that had to be confirmed by the church, who prayed until God gave them the same message.

Friesen seems to be of the opinion that the Holy Spirit cannot speak in such a mystical way, or at least that it cannot be objectively verified. This is a problem if it is true; especially since Romans 8:16 says, "The Holy Spirit bears witness with our spirit that we are children of God." How does God communicate this message of assurance? It is given not by an audible voice but by the Holy Spirit's giving assurance to an individual's spirit.

In addition to the three passages mentioned above, at least two others should be added. First, Paul says to the elders of the Ephesian church, "Take heed to the flock over which the Holy Spirit has made you overseers" (Acts 20:28). It is clear that they were made elders by the direction and will of God. They did not merely decide to become elders because they thought it would be a good thing to do. The decision originated with God. Because we cannot simply and easily explain how this process works does not mean we have the right to deny it altogether.

In addition, Romans 10:14–15 describes the process of how people hear the gospel and come to faith in Christ. Part of the process is hearing the gospel preached. Then the question is raised: "How shall they preach except they be sent?" If they are sent, who sends them? The obvious answer is, God does. If God sends them, there must be a way that He tells them to go.

In conclusion, the "wisdom" position says that a person uses the wisdom God gives him to decide what God's will is for his life (as long as it does not contradict Scripture). This includes the decision of whether to go into the ministry. The weakness of the wisdom position is this. Even though Friesen can point out weaknesses in the traditional view of a calling to ministry, there are no clear-cut cases in Scripture where anyone on the basis of his own wisdom decided to go into the ministry without some special leading of the Holy Spirit.

It might also be noted that under this approach the one who chooses to be a minister without a specific call is also free to depart the ministry at any time if he no longer has the desire to pursue it. Against this view are the following points: (1) A desire to seek the office of pastor does not automatically qualify one for the office. (2) First Timothy 3:1 only says that to desire such an office is a "good" thing. It does not state any further conclusions. Stringent qualifications are set forth in the succeeding verses to limit the office to those who meet the qualifications. (3) It is also very interesting that some who take this position believe that one cannot be saved without being "called" by the Spirit, yet once saved that person can decide to go into the ministry without any specific call.

The Universal View

In addition, there is the view that all Christians are called to serve God. Therefore, there is no group that is set aside for special service. This approach is found in Os Guinness's *The Call*. Guinness argues that to narrow "the sphere of calling" to those who are called to a spiritual ministry is to flagrantly pervert biblical teaching.[6] He says a holistic understanding of calling needs to be restored. He explains his view in the following manner:

> We are not primarily called to do something or
> go somewhere; we are called to Someone. We are
> not called first to special work but to God. The key
> to answering the call is to be devoted to no one
> and to nothing above God himself.[7]

While many might agree with Guinness's emphasis that every believer has a call to serve God, many would take issue with his statement: "There is not a single instance in the New Testament of God's special call to anyone into a paid occupation or into the role of a religious professional."[8] One might argue that the term *religious professional* would be considered a derogatory term to anyone who is called to a life of ministry to others. Most ministers would not consider themselves professionals. However, if the term is meant to apply to anyone who is paid to minister on a full-time basis, there are sufficient examples of religious professionals who were supported by New Testament churches. First Corinthians 9:1–18 is about this very thing. It is summed up in verse 14: "Even so the Lord has commanded that those who preach the gospel should live from the gospel." Paul instructs Timothy on this matter in 1 Timothy 5:17: "Let the elders who rule well be counted worthy of double honor." The word *honor* probably refers to financial support because it is connected with verse 18, which says, "The laborer is worthy of his wages."

The Traditional View

Finally, there are many Bible scholars both past and present who believe that Scripture indicates that a pastor must be called of God for that ministry. James M. George, writing in *Rediscovering Pastoral Ministry,* which is edited by John MacArthur, concludes that God calls selected men to serve and these must have assurance that God has called them.[9] The leader is no different from other members, except that God chose him and gifted him to do the work.[10] Speaking about the pastor, W. A. Criswell says, "The first and foremost of all the inward strengths of the pastor is the conviction, deep as life itself, that God has called him to the ministry. If this persuasion is unshakeable, all other elements of the pastor's life will fall into beautiful order and place."

There is no doubt that the Bible presents the minister as a God-called man. In the Old Testament no prophet dared assume the sacred office by himself. God had to call him (Deut. 18:20; Jer. 23:30; Isa. 6; Jer. 1:4–10). Ministers in the New Testament are always spoken of as designated by God (Acts 10:28; Col. 4:17).[11]

Edwin Lutzer supports the necessity of a special call to pastor, citing Paul's charge to Timothy in 1 Timothy 4:2–5. It is summed up with the command, "Fulfill your ministry." He observes that "those without a sense of calling tend to have horizontal vision. They lack the urgency of Paul, who said, 'Necessity is laid on me.'"[12] One must agree with Edwin Lutzer that there is more than just a vocational choice here that a man can take or leave. This urgency to preach is also seen in Paul's statement to the Corinthians: "Necessity is laid on me; yes woe is me if I do not preach the gospel!" (1 Cor. 9:16). Paul felt as though he had no choice but to preach since God called him.

Lutzer describes the call as "an inner conviction given by the Holy Spirit and confirmed by the word of God and the body of Christ."[13] It is difficult to see how a person could survive in the ministry if he felt it was solely his decision.

C. H. Spurgeon in *Lectures to My Students* spends an entire chapter on the call to the preaching ministry. He begins by citing Paul's statement in 2 Corinthians 4:1: "Since we have this ministry." Expounding on this text, he says, "No man may intrude into the sheepfold as an under-shepherd; he must have an eye to the chief Shepherd, and wait His beck and command."[14] From whom does one receive this ministry? It must be from God.

In addition to the precedents of the prophets in the Old Testament and the apostles in the New Testament, there is another important passage in Romans which bears on this subject. In Romans 10 Paul speaks of people calling upon the Lord to be saved. Then he says: "And how shall they call on Him in whom they have not believed? And how shall they believe in Him of whom they have not heard? And how shall they hear without a preacher? And how shall they preach unless they are sent?"

The last question is very important to this discussion. The obvious answer is that preachers must be sent, and the strong implication is that God sends them.

Confirmation of the Call

The Inward Call

The call is usually discussed under two headings: the inward call, which is God's call to a particular individual; and the outward call, which is God's confirmation of the individual's call through the local assembly of believers. The inward call may begin with either an intense desire or a profound conviction that God has chosen one to serve Him in a special way. Some argue that a person does not need a special call to the office of pastor-elder-bishop. The text is often cited, "If any desire the office of bishop he desires a good work" (1 Tim. 3:1). If someone has the desire and possesses the necessary gifts, then on that basis he may decide to become a pastor. However, is the inclination or desire to serve a call? Certainly not. One may perhaps desire the office for less than biblical reasons. Pure motivations do not guarantee that God is involved in the decision.

Those who were called in the Old Testament, such as prophets, for special offices did not always have a desire to serve, but they did have a profound and clear conviction that God had called them and they could not escape it. Jonah, for example, tried to run from God's call to go to Nineveh.

How does a man know he is called of God? First, there is the secret inner call known only to the minister himself. Does the person have a strong desire to serve God in the ministry? Is there evidence of the calling of the Holy Spirit in one's life? If one has this desire and believes God is calling him, then he should begin to examine himself to make sure he is hearing the right message. Thomas Oden lists questions one should ask oneself. Here are some of them:

1. Is this desire occasional or persistent?
2. Are there obvious blockages or irreversible encumbrances?
3. How much am I willing to give up?
4. How spiritually mature am I?
5. Can I stand alone, accountable before God?
6. Have I consulted with others concerning their perception of my potential gifts for ministry?[15]

Oden suggests that anyone who is resistant to this sort of soul-searching might not be a good candidate for the pastoral office. All of these questions involve judgments that have to be made and are therefore somewhat subjective—except one. When there are things in one's history that disqualify one from serving, subjective feelings should not override the qualifications given in Scripture. These qualifications will be discussed later, but they are summed up in one word: *blameless*.

The Outward Call

In order to verify one's call, one who feels led into the pastoral ministry should seek the counsel of the church body. As John Calvin put it, "A true minister of the church" should consider the objective or external call of the church and the secret inner call conscious only to the minister himself.[16] The purpose of this outward call is to confirm the inward call by deliberate testing and assessment. It should not be done in a hasty manner (1 Tim. 5:22).

The call to the ministry begins with the strong conviction from within a person that God is calling him for the ministry. He should also have a strong desire to glorify God and see the salvation of lost souls. However, the call must rest on a wider base than just a man's testimony that he felt God call him and he had a great desire to answer the call. It must also be evident that he possesses the necessary gifts and qualifications for the ministry. It is possible that a person could be mistaken about his own abilities. Those who know him best in the church should be able to advise him.

Francis Wayland says this concerning ministry: "We may frequently mistake our motives. We may overrate our capacity. We may thus run before we are sent. Hence we frequently see men in the ministry who have manifestly mistaken their calling, who are useless as preachers, while they might have been very useful in some other situation."[17]

If a man's fellow believers can confirm his call, then he can proceed with confidence into the ministry. This is what the ceremony called ordination is—public confirmation of an inner call and giftedness for ministry.

Some of the questions that should be asked to verify one's call are these:

1. Do others recognize my gifts and abilities in this area?

2. Have others asked me to serve in a leadership capacity?

3. Have others encouraged me to preach or teach?

4. Have some suggested I should consider the ministry?

5. Has God blessed my efforts in this area?

Finally, it should always be remembered that the call to be a pastor originates with God. (1) It began with God's creation of each individual. God has supplied the spiritual gifts (especially the gift of teaching) and the intellectual and social abilities necessary to be able to complete such a ministry. (2) It is God who by His Spirit places the desire to minister in a man's heart and calls him to surrender to a life of service.

In addition, (3) the candidate must have a lifestyle characterized by moral integrity and a commitment to continue in it. Any kind of moral failure is disastrous for effective spiritual ministry as a pastor. He must be "blameless." (4) The call must be confirmed by others. Anyone who goes ahead when godly people are pointing out problems with his suitability for the ministry needs to seriously reconsider the call.

3

The Role of the Pastor-Elder

One factor that becomes clear as one studies the New Testament church is that there was a great deal of organization necessary to accomplish the things the early church did.

Some of the evidences of a developed organizational structure are these:

1. They had a moderator, James, who was not one of the twelve apostles (Acts 15). As Saucy points out, this shows evidence of a change from apostolic leadership in this local church to another form.[1]

2. They knew the number of members they had (Acts 2:11; 4:4). Someone had to be responsible to count them.

3. They had regular meetings on the first day of the week (Heb. 10:25; 1 Cor. 16:2; Acts 20:7; John 20:19, 26).

4. In Jerusalem they met daily both publicly and in homes (Acts 2:42, 47; 20:7). This probably had to be coordinated by someone.

5. There were prayer meetings (Acts 2:42, 47; 12:5ff.).

6. The Lord's Supper was practiced (Acts 2:42, 46). Someone had to prepare for it and preside over its celebration in each house.

33

7. They practiced church discipline (Acts 5; 1 Cor. 5:4). Their procedure was probably based on Jesus' statements in Matthew 18:15–17.

8. They took up money for the poor in their midst as well as for other needy churches (1 Cor. 16:2–3; 2 Cor. 8:1–6; 9:1–7; Acts 2:45; 4:32–37; 6:1–3). If all these collections were being taken, someone had to administer the funds. In Acts 6 the first deacons were chosen for one part of this ministry, to give money to widows who were in need. First Timothy 5:9ff. also gives instructions about the care of widows.

9. Paul commanded that "all things should be done decently and in order" (1 Cor. 14:40). It is very difficult to have order without any organization. He adds that contentiousness was not part of the "custom" of the churches (1 Cor. 11:16).

10. Finally, the church sent out letters of commendation for saints who moved to new locations. Letters were sent for Apollos (Acts 18:24–28) and for Phoebe (Rom. 16:1–2).

The general practice of letters of recommendation is also found in 2 Corinthians 3:1–3. Modern-day churches continue this practice. In the New Testament, however, there is no practice of sending letters for those who were not faithful to the Lord and His church.

These indications of specific organization in the early church serve to demonstrate that the structure of the church was much more complicated than most people understand. One might ask, "If all these activities and functions were being performed, why is there not more direction given about how the church should be organized?" The answer is this. When directions are given, they must be followed exactly as Scripture says. The general principles are modeled for us. Details that are not given leave us free to adapt the structure to any given context.

Mayer divides the role of the elder into four categories: (1) overseeing and shepherding, (2) governing and leading, (3) preaching and teaching, and (4) relieving and healing. He views overseeing as basic to all four of the categories.[2] William Barclay concludes that the functions of the elder fall into only two main categories: administration and instruction.[3] While all such divisions are artificial, they are helpful in getting a good idea of all that is included in the role of the pastor-elder. Mayer points out that at least seventeen different functions can be listed for this office, which is good reason this ministry can be called "hard work."[4]

George adds a third category, pastoral duties, to Barclay's two. This seems to be the best option for understanding the pastor's role. His duties can be divided into these three functions: (1) instructional, equipping the saints; (2) pastoral, taking care of the flock; (3) administrative, overseeing the saints.[5]

In some ways these functions overlap, but in other ways they are distinct. They provide a structure for organizing a study of the pastor's role.

Instructional Duties

Perhaps the most important job of the pastor is that of teacher. Speaking of the roles of administration and instruction, Lightfoot says, "The work of teaching must have fallen to the elders from the very first and have assumed greater prominence as time went on."[6] The reasons for this conclusion are manifold. First there is Paul's discussion of spiritual gifts in Ephesians 4. One of the gifts God gives to the church is pastor, or teacher (v. 11). In this passage *teacher* is part of the name of the office. God creates such individuals to equip "the saints for the work of ministry." The pastor is to "edify" (strengthen) the body of believers. He is to do this by teaching the Word of God. He should train them until they become spiritual adults who are fully mature in Christ. If taught well, they will not be carried away by false doctrine or by the "craftiness of deceitful plotting" (Eph. 4:14).

A second vignette is found in Acts 6:1–4. Because of the growth of the church and the many demands placed on the apostles, they called a church meeting to discuss the problem.

Their assessment of the situation is found in verse 2: "It is not desirable that we should leave the word of God and serve tables." The point is not that the apostles were too good to minister to the church in this way but that it was not good for the church for them to be distracted from their primary function. They needed to keep the main thing the main thing. They said, "But we will give ourselves continually to prayer and the ministry of the word." The whole church suffers when the pastoral leadership is not spending time with God in prayer and the study of God's Word. This is the spiritual food they are to give out to the congregation.

One may ask, "Why can the church member not study for himself?" He can and should. However, the pastor should be able to help others to go deeper into the Word as he matures in Christ. One of the reasons God blessed the church in Jerusalem in the days after Pentecost is that they "continued steadfastly in the apostle's doctrine and fellowship, in the breaking of bread, and in prayers" (Acts 2:42). This is a must if a church is going to become mature in Christ.

A third reason to believe that teaching is the first priority of the ministry is found in the list of qualifications for bishops in 1 Timothy 3. Most of the qualifications have to do with the person's character. However, at least one spiritual gift is required. That gift is the gift of teaching. The pastor may have many gifts, but he must be "able to teach" (v. 2).

Another reason for pastors to emphasize teaching in their ministry is the Great Commission (Matt. 28:19–20). Jesus said, "Go therefore and make disciples of all the nations, baptizing them in the name of the Father and of the Son and of the Holy Spirit, teaching them to observe all things that I have commanded you." The verb *make disciples* means to make them "learners." They are to be "baptized" and "taught." Who is to teach them? As it has been pointed out previously, the pastor is called to be the "teacher" of the church.

Hopefully, he will not be the only one in the church who has this gift. Many others may have this gift, but the pastor is the "overseer" who makes certain they are being properly taught in the things of Christ.

Another little snapshot of the church, recorded in Acts 11, demonstrates the importance of teaching in the spiritual development of a congregation. The church at Antioch had had a great influx of new believers, and the church at Jerusalem sent Barnabas to check out the situation. He was pleased with what had happened there and encouraged them to "continue in the Lord" and to become "disciples of Jesus." Realizing he needed help with the job, he went to Tarsus and enlisted Saul to come and help disciple them (v. 25). Acts says that for a "whole year" they met with the church and "taught a great many people" (v. 26). The interesting thing is the following comment

Luke makes about the result of their teaching: "The disciples were first called Christians at Antioch."

Yet another line of evidence supports the contention
that teaching is the primary role of the pastor. When Jesus
spoke with Peter after the resurrection, He asked Peter
three times, "Do you love me?" (John 21:15–17). After
Peter's three replies, Jesus gave these commands: (1) "Feed
my lambs"; (2) "Tend my sheep"; (3) "Feed my sheep."
This motif of feeding the flock is a common one in the
New Testament. What does it mean? The meaning is fairly
obvious, but in case anyone has a problem understanding
it, Peter himself gives us the answer clearly in his first epistle: "As newborn babes, desire the pure milk of the word,
that you may grow thereby" (2:2). The spiritual food for
the believer is the Word of God. It was first the responsibility of the apostles to teach the brethren. As the church
increased, the responsibility for teaching was conferred on
the elders, who were the pastor-teachers of the churches.

Paul also emphasizes the importance of pastoral teaching. He instructs Timothy to give attention to three things
(1 Tim. 4:13). The first is "reading." The reference is not
just reading in general but reading of Scripture in the
worship services. This was important because few people
had copies of Scripture, so the only time they could hear it
read was at church. One may argue that it is not necessary
now because everyone has a Bible. However, it is still
necessary, because few actually read it.

The second is "exhortation." The word *exhortation* has
more than one emphasis. It can refer to "encouragement."
In other words, he was to cheer them on in their walk with
Christ. In addition, *exhortation* can mean an "appeal."
Timothy was to appeal to them—to earnestly beg them—
to continue to be faithful. Finally, *exhortation* includes

"comfort." Another task of the pastor is to comfort those who are in sorrow.

Besides "reading" and "exhortation," Paul tells Timothy to give attention to "doctrine." The word *doctrine* means "teaching." He is to emphasize teaching in his ministry.

In the next chapter Paul comes back to the matter of the pastor's role in teaching. He gives this instruction in 1 Timothy 5:17: "Let the elders who rule well be counted as worthy of double honor, especially those who labor in the word and doctrine."

It is important to look closely at this verse to see exactly what it is saying. Some have seen it as dividing elders or pastors into two groups, those who rule and those who teach. If this be the case, it is the only place in Scripture where such a division of labor is even mentioned. What it more likely means is that there is a distinction between those who "rule well" and those who do not. Those who do should be considered worthy of more pay (see verse 18). The second part of the verse expands on the first part. "Especially those who labor in the word and teaching" further qualifies the statement about those who "rule well." It is not about those who "teach" as opposed to those who "rule." This is a false dichotomy.

There is no such thing in the New Testament as an elder who only rules and does not teach. The "ones who rule well" and the "ones who labor in the word" are the same ones. The word translated "labor" here is *kopiao*. This is not the ordinary word for "work" *(ergazomai)*, which means to be active or busy and refers to work in general.[7] The word used here, in contrast, refers to a special category of work: hard work, labor, toil to the point of becoming weary.[8] As Solomon said long ago, "Much study is wearisome to the flesh" (Eccles. 12:12). Perhaps this is why so few do it, but one cannot "rule well" without "laboring" in the Word in order to be able to teach and thereby feed God's flock.

This point is further emphasized by Paul in his second epistle to Timothy. He gives Timothy a charge. He says, "Preach the word! Be ready in season and out of season. Convince, rebuke, exhort, with all longsuffering and teaching."

Two things stand out here. First, there is an urgency about this business of preaching and teaching God's Word. It has eternal consequences for good if done properly. One cannot afford to be careless or lukewarm, missing good opportunities to mention the faith. Second, he must "convince" (reprove) people of the truth of his claims by argumentation and teaching.[9] To convince people by careful arguments takes adequate preparation—in other words, hard work.

Finally, there is the matter of spiritual gifts. It has been mentioned that Ephesians 4:11 lists the pastor-teacher as one of God's gifts to the church. God gave "some to be pastor-teachers." In this passage individual apostles, prophets, evangelists, and pastors are God's gifts to the church. Compare this with spiritual gifts mentioned in other passages, shown in the chart on the next page.

In comparing the lists, one important observation should be made. Two of the lists emphasize the gifts or spiritual abilities God gives. The last two lists emphasize the categories of people God has given to the church. Some argue that pastor-elders do not have to have any particular spiritual gift.[10] Since some assume that there will be many elders in each church, then each should practice the gift he has, whatever it is. Some will have the gift of teaching. However, it should also be noted that there is a

Spiritual Gifts in Selected Passages

Romans 12:6–8	1 Corinthians 12:8–10	1 Corinthians 12:28–30	Ephesians 4:11
Prophecy	Word of Wisdom	Apostles	Apostles
Ministry	Word of Knowledge	Prophets	Prophets
Teaching	Faith	Teachers	Evangelists
Exhortation	Healings	Miracles	Pastor-Teachers
Giving	Miracles	Healings	
Leading	Prophecy	Helps	
Showing Mercy	Discerning of Spirits	Administrations	
	Tongues	Tongues	
	Interpretation of Tongues	Interpretation of Tongues	

connection made in Romans 12 and 1 Corinthians
12:8–10 between the gift that has been given and the
person who has it. Teachers should exercise the gift of
teaching, and the only position listed that is connected
with teaching is pastor-teacher. Evangelists and prophets,
for example, may teach us some things, but their gift is
separate from teaching. The question is, Does God endow
people with spiritual gifts which are necessary for the
work He intends for them to do? The answer is yes. Paul
told Timothy "to stir up the gift of God which is in you"
(2 Tim. 1:6). God does not call people to specific ministries for which He has not equipped them.

Pastoral Duties

The office of pastor-elder includes a second category of
responsibility. The role of the pastor-elder includes several
functions that come under the general heading, *pastoral
duties.*

The title of this category comes naturally from the many
references to a church as a flock of sheep that needs a
shepherd (cf. Acts 10:28; 1 Pet. 5:2). All of the functions
of a pastor in some way come under this category—hence
the title pastor (shepherd). For instance, teaching could be
included under "pastoral duties" because it involves feeding the flock. Administrative duties also relate to the care
of the sheep. Because sheep are not independent travelers,
someone must guide them and make plans for their care.
One reason for not putting all the categories under the
heading of pastoral duties is that the comparison of the
church to a flock of sheep is not the only figurative
description of the church and its leadership. The subject is
larger than just one illustration, as will be demonstrated
later.

Let us look again at Paul's message to the Ephesian elders. He says, "Take heed to yourselves and to all the flock" (Acts 20:28). This means to "turn one's mind to something," "to pay attention."[11] Focus your attention on yourself first. This does not mean to be selfish but to be concerned about your own spiritual condition. If the shepherd is not spiritually alert and walking closely with Christ, he will be of little help to the sheep. In the following verse it becomes clear why the shepherd should be focused and paying close attention to his sheep. Paul warns that "savage wolves will come in among you, not sparing the sheep." Of course he is not speaking about four-legged wolves and the physical welfare of the sheep; he is talking about the spiritual welfare of the church. In verse 30 he warns them that "men will speak perverse things, to draw away the disciples after themselves." From whence will these men come? They will come "from among yourselves." A shepherd who does not constantly guard against the encroachment of false doctrine will lose some of his sheep to false teaching.

Jesus also speaks about this aspect of pastoring in the sermon about the good shepherd (John 10:1–30). He presents a contrast between a real shepherd and a hireling. The shepherd leads the sheep out to find pasture. In other words, he nourishes them. The big difference between a real shepherd and a hireling becomes apparent when the wolf comes. The hireling flees, but the good shepherd protects his sheep even to the point of sacrificing his own life (John 10:11–12).

A great example of a good shepherd in the Old Testament is David. His own testimony is this: "Your servant used to keep his father's sheep, and when a lion or a bear came and took a lamb out of the flock, I went out after it and struck it, and delivered the lamb out from its mouth; and when it arose against me, I caught it by its beard, and struck and killed it" (1 Sam. 17:34–35). David's courage and faithfulness to the literal flock was part of the testing that prepared him to lead God's real flock, Israel. Courage is an absolute necessity for a pastor.

The pastoral epistles, written to Timothy and Titus, have a lot to say about the subject of protecting the flock from false doctrine. Some will argue that Timothy and Titus are not specifically given the title elder or pastor (which is true) and therefore these Scriptures cannot be included in a discussion of pastor-elders. However, if they were not serving as elders in their respective churches, Timothy at Ephesus and Titus in Crete, what position in the church did they have? Mayer concludes, for example, that they were "not elder-overseers but apostolic legates."[12] They had authority to direct the churches because they represented Paul the apostle rather than because they held any office themselves. This is unlikely because the churches had had pastor-elders to lead them for about twenty years by this time (ca. A.D. 63–67).

Timothy and Titus did not simply go to their churches, deliver Paul's message, stay a short time, and then leave. They apparently were there to stay for an undetermined amount of time. Several years may have elapsed between 1 and 2 Timothy. If he was still in Ephesus after so long a time, he was certainly more permanent in the church there than if he had simply been a messenger (see Titus 3:12 also). In addition, the ministries they were told to perform were the same basic duties that a pastor-elder performs. It has also been pointed out that at least two of the apostles also called themselves elders (2 John 1; 3 John 1). First Peter 5:2 has Peter calling himself an elder, and the date is somewhere in the same period as John's epistles (ca. A.D. 63). Therefore, there is little reason for denying that Timothy and Titus were serving as pastors. There is no other office mentioned in the New Testament that they could have held.

According to Plummer, the first epistle to Timothy treats three subjects: "Christian doctrine; Christian worship; and the Christian ministry."[13] Hendrickson outlines the entire second letter to Timothy around the theme of sound doctrine (teaching). He says to "hold on to it," "teach it," "abide in it," and "preach it."[14] The primary function of a pastor is to teach the Word of God. Paul admonishes Timothy to sound doctrine (1 Tim. 1:3) because there are some who have already departed from the faith (1 Tim. 1:19–20), and there are more who will depart and teach ungodly doctrines (4:1–3). He charges Timothy to "guard what was committed to your trust" (6:20) and avoid false teaching.

The same message is reiterated in 2 Timothy. Timothy is to "hold fast the pattern of sound works which you have heard from me" (2 Tim. 1:13). Paul admonishes Timothy to "be strong in the grace that is in Christ Jesus" (2:1). He will need courage to deal with the false teaching of people like Hymenaeus and Philetus (2:17). There are also people like Alexander the coppersmith that Timothy will have to face (4:14). In other words, standing for Christ in Ephesus will be a difficult task. Someone must protect the flock from these false teachers and their ungodly teachings. This is the task of a shepherd, to protect the flock from spiritual wolves.

In order to protect the flock from false teaching, a pastor must know what good doctrine is and what it is not so he can recognize it and warn the church of its evils. The best way to protect the flock from false teaching is to feed them a steady diet of good teaching. As they mature in Christ, they will also be able to discern between good and evil.

In Titus, elder-bishops are instructed to do this very thing, "holding fast the faithful word as he has been taught, that he may be able, by sound doctrine, both to exhort and convict those who contradict" (Titus 1:9). Those who "contradict" are those who "profess to know God, but in work they deny Him" (1:1b). The problems addressed in Titus appear to be related to godly behavior or, rather, the lack of it. They are guilty of several types of immoral behavior, even to the point of being "abominable" (1:16). Paul gives instructions about being "chaste" (2:5), showing "integrity" (2:7), having "sound speech" (2:8), and "not pilfering" (2:10). It is not enough to profess to know Christ; there must be the evidence of a changed life. The false teachers in Crete needed to learn the lesson that sound doctrine leads to clean living. It is not clear what the origins of their false teaching were, but they were exposed as false by the low standard of morality that they encouraged. These are just some of the problems pastor-elders must face.

Although the role of the New Testament pastors was mostly spiritual in nature, they also had some responsibilities related to the physical needs of the congregation. There are three primary passages that deal with the pastors' involvement in issues. Acts 11:30 describes Paul and Barnabas bringing an offering from the church in Antioch to aid those who were suffering from a great famine that affected Judea in those days. The money was delivered to the elders at Jerusalem. Since all of Judea was affected, there may have been elders or pastors there from other cities to receive aid, but this is not known. The point is that the elders had the responsibility to see that the hungry were given care. However, they probably did not give out the money themselves because this was the expressed reason that the "deacons," or "almoners" as F. F. Bruce called them, were elected—to take care of the money for the poor and see that it was fairly distributed.[15] The elders were responsible for overseeing this ministry.

A second passage that refers to this pastoral ministry of elders is Acts 20:35. Paul says to the Ephesian elders, "I have showed you all things, how that so laboring you ought to support the weak, and to remember the words of the Lord Jesus, how he said, 'It is more blessed to give than to receive.'" The key word here is *weak* (*astheneo*). Who are they? Does it refer to those who are spiritually weak or those who are physically weak? The word may refer to someone who is sick, physically weak or feeble, morally weak or weak in faith (spiritually immature), or to someone who is weak economically (poor) or without influence.[16]

In this context it almost certainly refers to the support of those who are physically unable to care for themselves because of sickness or some other disability. The elders were to lead the church in giving them aid. Paul cites the fact that he worked hard so that he could provide for himself and those who worked with him. He then quotes the words of Jesus on the blessedness of giving. Therefore, there is little doubt the passage is referring to providing for physical needs. The pastor is to show concern and lead the church to help the needy. False teachers were known for their greed (1 Tim. 6:3–10); faithful pastors should focus on the needs of others. As Polhill says, "The minister is to be a servant, a giver, and not a taker."[17]

The third reference to elder-pastors and ministry to physical needs is James 5:14–16. The exact responsibility of the
elders, as well as the significance of their actions, have been
variously interpreted. Therefore, it is necessary to look
closely at the text. In verse 13, the believer who is being
persecuted is instructed to pray, but in verse 14, the sick
person is told to call for the elders to pray for him. Two different words are used to refer to the sick person. In verse
14 *asthenei* is used, and in verse 15 *kamnonta* is used. The
first word refers to one who is sick or ill. The second word
is more specific. It can refer to one who is "weary or worn
out by time." It can refer to someone who is hopelessly sick
or wasting away.[18] Mayer argues that since both of the
verbs are in the "present tense, and probably progressive,
they indicate that this person was making no progress
toward recovery."[19] The elders would be called in this case
because the sick person is not able to pray for himself.

Another issue is the anointing with oil. Some believe
that oil was used for its medicinal value.[20] An example in
the New Testament of this use is in the parable of the
Good Samaritan (Luke 10:34). When the Samaritan had
bandaged the man's wounds, he poured on "oil and
wine." An Old Testament example is Isaiah 1:6, where it
is used as a treatment for wounds, bruises, and sores on
the body. Others believe that the anointing was ceremonial
or symbolic.[21] In this case the oil would have acted as a
stimulant to faith. It was the "prayer of faith" that "saves"
the person in either case, not the medicine or the act of
anointing. This does not mean that a person should not
take medicine. All the means for health that God has pro-
vided should be used in addition to prayer. For instance, in
Isaiah 38:21, when King Hezekiah prayed for God to
extend his life (38:2), he was instructed by Isaiah to apply

a "poultice on the boil" so he would recover (see also Mark 6:12–13 and 1 Tim. 5:23).

There is one more possible way to interpret this passage. Verse 15 adds that there is a possibility that the sick person has "committed sins."[22] If this be the case, then confession is necessary before one prays for healing. In the final analysis it is God who decides whether healing occurs. It must be according to his will (1 John 5:14). It is impossible for human beings to manipulate the will of God.

However, when one looks at the interpretation of these verses, one thing is clear. Elder-pastors have the responsibility to pray for the sick when they are called upon to do so. There is no mention here that a gift of healing is necessary. In fact, there is no mention in the New Testament of elders being required to have any particular gift except the gift of teaching. They minister and pray because they are the spiritual leaders of the church. Neither does this mean that other believers are exempt from praying for the sick just because they are not pastors. The only requirement in James 5 for prayer to be acceptable to God is that it must come from a "righteous" person.

The other ministries that a pastor performs, such as witnessing in the community and helping those with various kinds of needs, he performs not because they are specific ministries assigned to him by Scripture but because these things are commanded for all Christians.[23] He does them in obedience to the Lord and as an example to other believers. He cannot expect his congregation to be faithful in witnessing if they do not see him being faithful to share the gospel. By example and by word, he should teach them to do the same. If he has no concern for the needy, it will not be a priority in the ministry of the church either.

In summary, the primary pastoral duty in the elder-pastor's role is to protect the flock from false teaching. As Hebrews 13:17 says, "They watch out for your souls, as those who must give account." In addition, the pastor is to pray for the sick, especially those with serious problems, when called upon, and he is to be generous and lead the church in helping those with basic physical needs.

Administrative Duties

One of the basic functions of the pastor-elder is that of "overseeing."[24] Mayer includes overseeing with shepherding. However, these two terms are not entirely parallel. The word *episkopos* means "bishop" or "overseer." This title is interchangeable with the title *elder* or *pastor*.[25] A shepherd does "oversee" a flock of sheep. This could include all the functions of guiding, feeding, protecting, and caretaking. Today, however, to many in the church *shepherding* has a different connotation than *overseeing*. Shepherding is connected primarily with taking care of the physical needs of the church, such as visiting the sick, and comforting the bereaved. Overseeing would be primarily associated with "guiding" and "supervising" the work of the church.

Some argue that the term *bishop* is only descriptive of the function of the pastor-elder; it is not an official title.[26] While it is descriptive of the pastor's role, it is used as a title too. In Philippians 1:1 Paul addresses the "bishops and deacons." The qualifications for the "position of a bishop" are given in 1 Timothy 3:1–7. Support for this use of *episkopos* is found in the Greek papyri of pre-Christian times and later. In Rhodes, for example, members of the city council were called "bishops." The officials of the temple there were also called "bishops."[27] In the writings of Philo, Moses is referred to as a "bishop" also.[28] Arndt says that an *episkopos* is one who has a "definite function or a fixed office within a group."[29] He is a superintendent or guardian.

In this context of the church, the question is, What does he superintend and what does he guard? As pastor (bishop) he is the chief officer in the church. Overseeing implies that he has administrative responsibility for the entire operation of the church. He is not responsible for doing all the work but for seeing that it is done and done properly. Sheep are not independent travelers. It is his responsibility to guard them from false doctrine—to keep them from going astray and to keep them going in the right direction. In order to perform this task, he must have the authority from God to do it. He is not, however, to lead the flock by fiat but by being an example to the flock.

A second word describes the administrative function of the pastor-elder. In Titus 1:7 he is described as "a steward of God." By the very nature of the office, he is to manage the things of God. The word used here is *oikonomon*. In Luke 12:42 and 16:1–8 this term refers to the manager of an estate. The *oikonomon* was a servant who supervised the other servants. Because of his position he was held responsible for his master's business. Paul uses this term to refer to himself in 1 Corinthians 4:1–2. Paul and the other ministers who had been there (Peter and Apollos, 1 Corinthians 3:22; Sosthenes, 1:1) were "stewards of the mysteries of God." The "mysteries" of God refers to those things revealed which were once secret but have now been revealed to the church (Eph. 3:3–5). His job in regard to the "mysteries" was to safeguard the message by passing it on clearly and completely to the church. The steward will be judged by only one criterion—faithfulness (1 Cor. 4:2).

The use of the word *steward* has two different emphases in the New Testament. The steward is to safeguard the message to see that it is passed on and not corrupted. He is also to oversee the work of the other servants and give an account to the master.

The third term which is associated with the administrative duties of the pastor-elder is *proistemi*, which is usually translated "rule" in the King James Version. In secular Greek literature it can refer to one who "presides over a meeting." It is used to refer to the head of a guild (a group of craftsmen) or to the "head man of a village."[30] It literally means to "stand before" or "put before." In reference to groups like a church, it would mean to "preside," "rule," or "govern."[31] Arndt adds that the word means "be at the head (of), rule, direct."[32]

In the New Testament, *proistemi* is used eight times. Six of these uses refer in some way to the duties of church leaders. One of the qualifications given in 1 Timothy 3:4 for the position of bishop is the ability to "rule his own house well." He must show his ability to govern, administrate, and lead his own household. If there are problems there, if he does not show his leadership ability in the home, how will he be able to "take care of" the church of God? Notice the connection between "ruling" or "leading" and "taking care of." It shows that there should be a nurturing relationship between the pastor and the flock. The same word is also used to describe the qualifications of a deacon. It says the candidates for deacons must "rule" (govern, lead) their "children and their own houses well." The proving ground for church leaders is the home.

Later in 1 Timothy 5:17 there are directions to the church about the treatment and reward of elders. Ruling (governing, leading) "well" is connected with "laboring" (working hard) in the Word and teaching. Ruling or lead-ing well cannot be separated from "laboring." Teaching effectiveness is increased by working at it. Knowledge of the word is not gained by osmosis but by diligent study. Without knowledge of the Word one cannot rule well. Effectiveness at teaching is also increased by the personal example of being faithful at one's job day by day. Such devotion to the task does not go unnoticed by God or men.

First Thessalonians 5:12 discusses how the congregation should treat its leaders. They should "know" them (v. 12) and "esteem" them (v. 13). In particular they should respect those who: (1) "work hard among you," (2) "stand in front of you" (lead), and (3) "admonish you." This last word literally means "putting sense into the heads of people."[33] In other words, they are to follow leaders who teach, lead the way, and work hard. This verse pictures a leader who rules not by coercion but by persuasion and example.

There is one other use of *proistemi* in the New Testament. In Paul's list of spiritual gifts in Romans 12, there is a word to those who rule (lead). Those who lead do so because they are gifted by God to do so. It is God's choice, not ours. Being called of God to be a pastor-elder involves the recognition of gifts given to the individual by God's grace (v. 6). Sometimes a person has gifts that may have remained dormant for years because he has not sur-rendered himself to Christ and allowed them to be used. The one who has the gift is commanded to lead "with dili-gence." This means literally "in haste" or "in earnest."[34] In other words, the leader should be serious about his task. He should have a sense of urgency about it because people are dying without Christ.

Conclusion

The role of the pastor-elder can be described under three separate headings. He is to be a teacher, a pastor, and a leader of the congregation. The primary job of the pastor is to teach the Word. This should be primary because it is the most emphasized function of the pastor in the New Testament. Preaching and exhortation are included under this function.

The second function is the pastoral role. This includes prayer in general and prayer for and visitation of the sick (when called). The pastoral function most often mentioned after teaching is guarding the flock against false teaching. This necessitates being able to detect false doctrine and expound and apply the cure of sound doctrine.

The third function of a pastor-elder is leadership. He is one who stands in front. He is the overseer, the steward, who is responsible to the Master for the spiritual well-being of the congregation. He must remember that he is also a servant who must give an account of his own stewardship.

Anything else the pastor does is done because he is a believer, not because he is pastor. He is not exempt from anything that all Christians are commanded to do. He is to give because all are to give. He is to witness because all are to witness. The difference is that the pastor-elder is to lead other believers by being an example to them. He is to model what a Christian should be.

4

The Qualifications for Pastor-Elders

Two passages in the New Testament list the qualifications of pastor-elder. A list is given in 1 Timothy 3:1–7 for any man who aspires to the office of bishop or overseer. A second list of qualifications is in Titus 1:6–9. These are given as guidelines to Titus by Paul as he seeks out those who should be appointed as elder-bishops. Most of the qualifications have to do with the candidate's character.

As James George has put it, "What he is is far more important than what he does."[1] Ministry is as much about what we are as what we do and say. For that reason Paul said to Timothy, "Meditate on these things; give yourself entirely to them, that your progress may be evident to all. Take heed to yourself and to the doctrine" (1 Tim. 4:15–16a). The leader who does not pay attention to his own spiritual development and health will soon be a detriment rather than a blessing to his flock. This principle is illustrated in Old Testament practice also. The high priest was himself "subject to weakness." Therefore, "he is required as for the people, so also for himself, to offer sacrifices for sins" (Heb. 5:2b–3).

Again, Saucy says, "Spiritual leadership without character is only religious activity, possibly religious business, or hypocrisy."[2] Character problems are at the heart of the pastor's qualification. Paul said to the Corinthians,

"Be imitators of me" (1 Cor. 4:16 NASB). Peter said, "Nor as being lords over those entrusted to you, but being examples to the flock" (1 Pet. 5:3). Many other texts echo the same idea of leaders leading by exhibiting a godly example (see Phil. 3:17; 4:9; 2 Thess. 3:9).

Henry Martyn, the great missionary, wrote in his journal, "The first great business on earth is the sanctification of my own soul."[3]

Most of the virtues listed in these two passages should be the goal of all believers to attain. As Mayer says, "Only those men who have attained and maintained them are qualified for overseership."[4] Pastors must be of the highest character to be effective in leading the church.

1 Timothy 3:1–7

Fifteen qualifications are listed in this passage. Many have attempted to categorize these fifteen in some way, but there is no general agreement on how they should be outlined. Two facts about them are obvious, however. (1) The first seven are presented in a positive manner, while the final eight are characteristically negative. (2) The first fourteen virtues relate primarily to those in the church, whereas the final requirement relates to those outside the church. Concerning this Hendrickson says, "The prospective overseer must have a favorable testimony from two groups: (a) insiders, that is, church members, and (b) outsiders, that is those who are outside the church."[5] While there is no clear delineation of categories in the text beyond the two mentioned, some organization will be helpful in getting a handle on what is required of a prospective pastor-elder. Homer Kent's outline is helpful for that purpose, so it will be used to clarify the requirements. The headings are: (1) general, (2) moral,

(3) mental, (4) personality, (5) domestic, (6) Christian experience, and (7) reputation.[6]

General Qualification

The first characteristic, "blameless," means "above reproach." It is probably to be an inclusive term that is used to sum up all of the requirements in one. The word originally meant "not to be laid hold of." It is used of a wrestler who does not give his opponent an opportunity to get a hold on him.[7] Accusations may be made against him, but no grounds for them exist.

Moral Qualification

The only requirement for the office of pastor-elder that is controversial is "husband of one wife." There are at least five views on this subject. One of them is entirely a Roman Catholic view.

Marriage-to-the-Church View. In this view the "one wife" is the church. The pastor must consider himself married to the church. About this view Kent says, "This is an obvious and rather clumsy attempt to protect the Romish doctrine of celibacy for priests. However, there is no warrant for spiritualizing this part of the passage when every other term in the list is understood literally."[8] It must be said that not even all Catholics follow this view.

Prohibition-of-Polygamy View. This view is appealing today to some because polygamy is not a problem in Western society; therefore, it does not cause any controversy over whether anyone qualifies for the ministry. The NIV translation of this verse implies by its wording that the qualification refers to polygamy: "The overseer must be . . . the husband of one wife." Polygamy was certainly not accepted in the first-century church. It hardly seems necessary even to say it.

Polygamy was illegal in the Roman Empire, and even though it still occurred among the heathen and some Jews, a pastor could not be considered "above reproach" if he practiced it.[9] Beyond this, if Scripture forbids polygamy for all Christians (1 Cor. 7:2), it certainly includes pastors. Polygamy is, undoubtedly, not the target of this phrase. Kelly says, "That the words are directed against either keeping concubines or polygamy, i.e. having more than one wife at a time" are "suggestions which are improbable in the extreme."[10]

Exclusion-of-Unmarried-Pastors View. Though this view is mentioned as a possibility by most commentators, no one seems to hold it or defend it.[11] This view is flawed on two counts. (1) Paul would not have to emphasize "one wife" if this were the case. He would only have to say that a pastor must have "a wife." (2) Paul himself saw nothing wrong with his unmarried state (1 Cor. 7:7–8, 17). In fact, he encourages others to be happy in their situation whether they are married or unmarried. (3) Paul was unmarried at the time he wrote, but he considered himself to be one of the elders (pastors). In 2 Timothy 1:6 he reminds Timothy of the gift that was in him "through the laying on of my hands." Add to that verse 1 Timothy 4:14, which says, "Do not neglect the gift that is in you . . . with the laying on of the hands of the eldership." Paul must have considered himself part of the group of elders who laid hands on Timothy. (4) One final point against this view is this. If "husband of one wife" is taken to mean a pastor-elder must have a wife, then "ruling their children and their own houses well" must be taken to mean that a pastor must have children. Otherwise there is no consistency in the interpretation.

Prohibition-of-Remarried-Widowers   View.   Simply stated, this means that a pastor may marry once, but if his wife dies, he may not marry a second time. Kent points out that this opinion is very common in Europe.[12] Plummer argues in favor of this view. His main arguments are these. (1) Among the heathen there was a special respect for the *univira,* the woman who was married to only one man in her lifetime. Therefore, he concludes, persons who did not remarry would be more respected in the community than those who did.[13] Against this point Keener demonstrates that men rarely abstained from a second marriage in this case and that this view more closely mirrors the sexual asceticism urged by the false teachers than Paul's own position.[14] (2) Plummer believes that a second marriage would be a sign of weakness even though it was lawful. Against this argument the question has been asked, "Why would it be any more a sign of moral weakness to remarry after the death of a spouse than to marry in the first place?" (3) Plummer also cites several of the church fathers such as Origin, Clement, and Tertullian who support his position.[15]

Against this view is the fact that this is the only moral requirement listed primarily for pastors. Is the remarriage of a widower the greatest sexual sin? Certainly not. It is not even mentioned anywhere else as a problem. Kent is correct when he says, "The chief weakness of this view is the lack of harmony with the tenor of Scripture teaching on the subject of marriage.

"Nowhere in Scripture (including Paul's epistles) is the remarriage of a widower after the death of the wife depicted as forbidden or even morally questionable."[16] The younger widows are advised to remarry (1 Tim. 5:14).

In the light of the advice in Genesis 2:18 and Romans 7:2 (death annuls the contract), there is no reason pastors who are widowers may not remarry "in the Lord."

Faithful-to-One's-Current-Wife View. In most commentaries more than one generation old, this view is not even discussed as a possibility. However, it has come to be accepted by some in recent times. Keener expresses his interpretation in this way: "Rather than forbidding remarriage to those whose marriages had ended, Paul may be emphasizing that they should have been faithful spouses during the marriage."[17] He says that "husband of one wife" here refers to "a faithful and loyal spouse who is a good current marital partner."[18] It would not, in his opinion, disqualify "a capable prophet or teacher because of a bad marriage many years ago, often before his or her conversion."[19] His supporting argument is that marriage to only one partner in a lifetime was never a qualification for leaders in the ancient world. On the other hand, marital fidelity was often required.

Lea and Griffin also support this position. They conclude, "It is better to see Paul having demanded that the church leader be faithful to his one wife. The Greek describes the overseer literally as a 'one-woman kind of man' ('faithful to his one wife,' NEB)."[20] According to this view, a divorced man can serve as a church leader, either as a pastor-elder or deacon, if he is thoroughly devoted to his present wife. The primary argument for this view would be that a man's preconversion sins should not be held against him. If this conclusion is correct, then Paul's emphasis is not to warn against divorce and remarriage, but to disqualify whoever is known to be flirtatious (interested in other women) from serving as a pastor or deacon.

There are several problems with this view. First, Keener's argument about what was required for leaders in the ancient world is extremely weak. Obviously, the moral standards and family commitments expected for Christian leaders were far beyond that of the world of that day. There is little ground for comparison. Second, the translation "one-woman kind of man" seems to bring the qualification down to its lowest common denominator. J. N. D. Kelly observes, "This is to squeeze more out of the Greek than it will bear."[21] Certainly a pastor-elder should not be flirtatious with other women, but this is not a qualification for a pastor—this is a requirement for all Christian men. Paul says to all, "Abstain from every form [appearance] of evil" (1 Thess. 5:22), and to Timothy, "Flee youthful lusts" (2 Tim. 2:22). Again it should be asked, "Is that the only moral requirement that sets the pastor apart from others?" Probably not.

There is another serious defect with this position. There are a lot of unanswered questions associated with it. If a remarried man is to be accepted as a pastor-elder, how long must he have been faithful to his new wife to qualify? Three months, a year, two years, five years? Will only those divorced before becoming a Christian be qualified, or will others qualify also? Will only those who were the "innocent party" qualify, or is the qualification broader? These questions are not addressed in Scripture, which leads to the conclusion that this option was not anticipated by the writers of the New Testament.

Perhaps the strongest argument against this view is found in 1 Timothy 5:9. The same phrase, "man of one woman" or "husband of one wife," is turned around to refer to widows who would be supported by the church. Here it reads "wife of one husband" or "woman of one man." In this case the verse clearly does not refer to being faithful to one's present husband because it refers to a widow. First Timothy 5:9 has generally been understood to refer to a woman who has had only one husband. If it clearly refers to a woman's past marital record and not to her present condition (having a reputation of being flirtatious, for instance), then how can the same phrase be differently understood when applied to pastors? One must conclude that this interpretation is not a suitable answer to the question of what "husband of one wife" means.

Prohibition-of-Divorce View. This view would interpret the phrase "husband of one wife" as a prohibition of divorce and any other kind of marital infidelity. This view can be supported for three reasons. (1) It is consistent with the historical background of the first-century Roman Empire. One of the two greatest social problems in the empire in those days was the high rate of divorce. Divorce could be obtained easily by both men and women under Roman law and by men under Jewish law. Kent points out, "When congregations were organized, the overseers were chosen from among mature men, who usually were married men with families . . . that is why this list of qualifications was necessary. Consequently, when men were to be considered for this office, there must be no record of divorce or any other marital infidelity in the candidate, even before his conversion."[22]

Otherwise, the church could be caught in a complicated or even embarrassing situation when reports about former wives, mistresses, illegitimate children, or children from other marriages came to light. Some might argue that since those things happened in the preconversion life, they should be forgiven and overlooked. It is true that Jesus' blood can make the vilest sinner clean, and all genuine converts are forgiven of sin and accepted into the body of Christ. It does not necessarily follow that all are then qualified to be pastors or deacons, regardless of what kind of past they have had. The matter of a person's reputation in the world cannot be overlooked (1 Tim. 3:7). For the church to have a moral impact on society, the highest standards should be upheld.

A second argument for this position is the teaching against divorce in other Scripture. Hultgren argues for this position because "remarriage after divorce was prohibited for all followers in the teachings of Jesus (Matt. 19:9; Mark 10:11–12; Luke 6:18) and Paul (1 Cor. 7:10–11). If that prohibition applies to all, much more does it apply in the Pastoral Epistles to those in positions of leadership."[23] According to Romans 7:2–3, the only thing which frees a person from the marriage contract is death. It reads: "For the woman who has a husband is bound by the law to her husband as long as he lives. But if the husband dies, she is released from the law of her husband. So then if, while her husband lives, she marries another man, she will be called an adulteress."

For this reason Christian marriage ceremonies for centuries past have included the pledge "till death do us part." Paul addresses in 1 Corinthians 7:11 cases where separation is either necessary or imposed by the other partner: "But even if she does depart, let her remain unmarried or be reconciled to her husband. And a husband is not to divorce his wife." It is clearly not the ideal in God's plan to get a divorce. Therefore, the pastor who is to be a role model for the congregation should not be divorced.

Paul is only repeating the teachings of Jesus on this issue. In Mark 10:11 Jesus said, "Whoever divorces his wife and marries another commits adultery against her."

The principle is that God has them "joined together" and they are now "one flesh." Even though they may be divorced according to the law, they are still "one flesh." So the conclusion according to this view is that if a man has two living wives, he has two wives and does not qualify to be a pastor-elder.

Some might argue that there is an exception clause in Matthew 19:9 ("except for sexual immorality"). The disciples were questioning Jesus about divorce and why Moses permitted it even though God had told them not to separate (19:6–7). Jesus said it was allowed because of the "hardness of your heart." He then repeats the same statement about divorce and remarriage being adultery "except for sexual immorality" *(porneia;* 19:8–9). Many have taken this to mean that adultery gives a person grounds for divorce and remarriage. However, few notice the reaction of the disciples to His statement. Their reply is, "If such is the case of the man with his wife, it is better not to marry" (v. 10).

Jesus then says, "All cannot accept this saying." In other words, whatever Jesus meant by His statement, He did not intend to make it easy to get a divorce. His disciples seemed to be shocked by His answer. This is interesting because one of the most common views of that time regarding divorce was that it was permitted on the grounds of adultery. Why did the disciples react so to His answer? Perhaps it was because Jesus meant divorce was permitted for adultery only during the period of Jewish betrothal, not after the actual wedding. This would make it a hard saying and evoke a reaction from them.

A third argument for the "not-divorced" view is its impact on the other qualifications for the office. Wiersbe argues that if the marriage has failed, a man cannot properly be said to have ruled his house well. He says:

"It's clear that a man's ability to manage his own marriage and home indicate ability to oversee a local church (1 Tim. 3:4–5). A pastor who has been divorced opens himself and the church to criticism from outsiders, and it is not likely that people with marital difficulties would consult a man who could not keep his own marriage together. I see no reason why dedicated Christians who have been divorced and remarried cannot serve in other offices in the church, but they are disqualified from being elders or deacons."[24]

The phrase "husband of one wife" is stated positively rather than negatively by Paul because it means more than just "not divorced." It means that a man is devoted to his wife. If he does not love her selflessly as the Scripture commands, he is not following the example of Christ and would, therefore, be a poor example to the church (Eph. 5:25ff.).

Mental Qualifications

Four qualifications for the pastor-elder concern his mental capabilities. The first is "temperate" *(nephalion)*. Its literal meaning is "sober, temperate; abstaining from wine, either entirely . . . or at least from its immoderate use."[25] About this word, Moulton and Milligan say, "In Greek Literature *nephalios* is used to refer either to altars at which only wineless offerings were made, or perhaps to cakes made in the form of an altar, free from all inclusion of wine."[26] Liddell and Scott also define the word in classical Greek usage to refer to persons drinking no wine, sober, or a drink without wine, such as those containing water, milk, or honey.[27] Josephus also uses the word with this meaning.[28]

Metaphorically, *sober* may denote one who is vigilant, calm, temperate, or free from excess that would cloud his spiritual judgment. Since wine is mentioned in the next verse, it is probably intended here to be taken in this sense. Barclay says the point here is that the "Christian must allow himself no pleasure or no indulgence that would lessen his Christian vigilance or soil his Christian conduct."[29]

The second word in this category is *sober-minded (sophrona)*. This word only occurs in the New Testament here and in Titus 1:8; and 2:2, 5. Arndt and Gingrich define *sophron* as meaning "prudent, thoughtful, self-controlled."[30] Barclay says it is really an untranslatable word, which means there is no single English word that gives its exact meaning. Besides the translations mentioned above, it has also been rendered "of sound mind," "discreet," "chaste," "having complete control over sensual desires."[31] It is derived from two words that mean "to keep one's mind safe and sound." It is discussed by many of the ancient philosophers, and the sum of the discussions is this: It refers to "the man who has every part of his nature under perfect control."[32] Barclay cites Jeremy Taylor who called it "reason's girdle and passion's bridle."[33] It describes a man in whom the Spirit of God has placed the mind of Christ.

The third mental qualification is to be "of good behavior." The Greek word is *kosmion,* which is used only once in the rest of the New Testament. In 1 Timothy 2:9 it is used to describe how women should dress. It is a companion word with the previous word *(sophron).* Barclay says, "If a man is *kosmios* in his outer conduct it is because he is *sophion* in his inner life."[34] The word means more than just good behavior; it means "orderly, honest, or virtuous." It is often used in ancient inscriptions to praise those who had lived an honorable and virtuous life.[35] It is related to *kosmeo,* to arrange, and *kosmos,* world, which is well ordered, not chaotic. Kent says, "The ministry is no place for the man whose life is a continual confusion of unaccomplished plans and unorganized activity."[36]

The final mental qualification is to be "able to teach." Since the primary function of a pastor-elder is teaching sound doctrine and refuting false teaching by expounding the Word of God, it is absolutely essential that a pastor be an effective teacher. The word *didaktikon* denotes one who is characterized by teaching. It is used only one other time in the New Testament. In 2 Timothy 2:25 it is used to describe the servant of the Lord (with special reference to Timothy who is also an elder) as one who was "able to teach." In this way the pastor-teacher is following the example of Jesus, who was called a "teacher come from God" (John 3:2) and who called Himself "your teacher, the Christ" (Matt. 23:8).

There is some disagreement over whether pastor-elders must have the spiritual gift of teaching. Mayer agrees that this qualification "demands a certain inherent mental capacity for teaching and assumes knowledge of what is taught."[37] However, he argues that this ability does not relate to the spiritual gift of teaching, but it is "only a natural aptitude for such." He is arguing from the position that some pastor-elders do not teach. However, Ephesians 4:7–12 speaks of the grace-gifts that God has given to the church. In that list teaching is linked with the office of pastor-elder. He is a teacher above all else. It is difficult to imagine that God would appoint men to the task of being a teacher without spiritually gifting them to do the job. Is the church to depend on natural ability only? The church needs more than that. It needs the enabling of the Spirit in its teaching. This is what Paul was speaking to Timothy about when he said, "Stir up the gift of God which is in you" (2 Tim. 1:6). The gift of teaching is indicated by his admonitions in verse 13 ("hold fast the pattern of sound words") and in chapter 2, verse 2 ("commit these to faithful men who will be able to teach others also"). Every pastor should have this gift.[38]

Personal Qualifications

Six qualifications fit this category. The first is "hospitable." The Greek term *philoxenos* is a compound of *philos* and *xenos* that literally means "loving strangers." The word is found in Titus 1:8 in the parallel list of elder qualifications and in 1 Peter 4:9, where it is commanded for all Christians. In that day there were traveling preachers and teachers as well as other believers who might pass their way. Inns of that time were usually ungodly places and sometimes dangerous as well. Since most Christian teachers and evangelists were poor, they were dependent on the hospitality of other believers. In his official capacity as a leader of the church, a pastor-elder had the duty of keeping his house open to strangers. All believers should be "given to hospitality" (Rom. 12:13) but especially the leaders.

The second personal requirement is to be "not given to wine." Literally, this means "not beside wine." Thayer translates *paroinos* as "one who sits long at his wine."[39] Kent interprets the phrase that the pastor "must not be a drinker."[40] Most agree that the phrase is teaching moderation in this regard, because wine was the usual beverage of that day. Barclay points out, however, that the normal mixture for table wine in that day was "two parts wine to three parts of water."[41] Drunkenness was a disgrace even in pagan society. Some pastor-elders in that time were total abstainers even though water was often impure. Paul had to urge Timothy to take a little wine for his stomach illnesses (1 Tim. 5:23).

The next qualification is to be "not violent" (*plekten*). It has been translated "not a striker" or "not given to blows." It refers to a man who is a "bully"[42] or a "bruiser, ready with a blow; a pugnacious, contentious, quarrelsome person."[43] The only other place it occurs in the New Testament is in the parallel passage, Titus 1:7. The pastor should not be one who is always ready for a fight, one who strikes back when he is challenged.[44]

The pastor-elder must be the opposite of a bully. He must be "gentle" *(epieike)*. This is another word that probably has no exact English equivalent, so it has been variously translated. Thayer lists its meaning as "yielding, gentle, kind."[45] Kelly uses the word *magnanimous* to describe its meaning. By this he means "the gracious condescension, or forbearingness, with which the Christian pastor should deal with his charges, however exasperating they may on occasion be."[46] He must be willing to surrender his own rights to avoid contention in the church. This word is also used in Philippians 4:5, Titus 3:2, and James 3:17. In these cases it is demanded of all believers, not just pastors. However, the pastor should be an example to all in this.[47]

The fifth personal qualification is to be "not quarrelsome" *(amachon)*. It means more than "not violent," but it means literally "averse to fighting."[48] This is not just a person who is not contentious but who loves peace. He keeps his temper under control. In Titus 3:2 it is translated "peaceable," and it is an admonition for all believers.

The last personal qualification for a pastor-elder is to be "not covetous." The Greek word is *aphilarguron,* which literally means "not a money lover." He must be one who keeps material things in their proper perspective because a love for money can lead to all kinds of evil (1 Tim. 6:10). The desire for money is both an attitude and an ambition. Jesus rebuked the Pharisees in Luke 16:13–15 for their love of money. Paul's admonition to all believers is to be content, both when there is abundance and when there is need (Phil. 4:11–12).

Domestic Qualifications

The candidate for "overseer" of a church must first be a good "ruler" (leader, manager) of his own household. It is assumed that he will be married and have children, though that is not required. As Mayer correctly observes, when the word *oikos* (house) is used to refer to a "household" rather than a physical structure where people live, it always refers to people. The emphasis is on how he oversees and leads the people in his house, who might include his wife, children, and possibly servants.[49] The second phrase, "having his children in submission with all reverence," seems to name the man's children as the primary area for testing. If the children exhibit obedience, discipline, and respect for his authority, that is proof of his ability to lead.

The last part of the phrase, "with all reverence," refers to how the pastor manages his household. It should be done with "dignity." If a father attempts to control his children solely by force rather than by winning their respect, he will usually treat church members in the same manner. Hendrickson describes the father's leadership in this way: "It must be done in such a manner that the father's firmness makes it advisable for a child to obey, that his wisdom makes it natural for a child to obey, and that his love makes it a pleasure for a child to obey."[50] Poor leadership in the home is a bad testimony, and it demonstrates a lack of competence for the pastoral office. Leadership or management skills are necessary to lead a household and even more necessary to lead a church. In short, a pastor must demonstrate skill in leading and managing people.

Christian Experience

The candidate for pastor-elder must not be a "novice." The term *neophuton* means "newly planted" or a "young plant." Hence, it refers to one who is a recent convert to the faith. This is the only use of this word in the New Testament, but Paul does use the same metaphor of planting and watering in 1 Corinthians 3:6 to refer to converting people to Christ. The danger of choosing a neophyte (new convert) for a position of leadership in the church is vividly described. He may become "puffed up with pride" or conceited. Literally, this means "wrapped up in smoke." He is "wrapped in the smoke of arrogance" as Hendrickson puts it,[51] which leads to a clouded mental state. This same sin brought judgment on the devil and will bring ruin to the novice also. The consequences will not only be disastrous for the novice but for the church as well. No matter how gifted and promising the new convert appears, he should not be elevated to this office until he has some maturity in Christ.

Reputation

The final qualification in this list is to be "a good testimony among those who are outside."

Among those who are not believers, he must have a good reputation. Those who have seen him at work in the secular world and who have associated closely with him often know more about his real character than do many of the church members. Beyond that, if the church is trying to win outsiders to the Lord and they choose a pastor who has a bad reputation with unbelievers, it will be difficult, if not impossible, to make an impact with them. Those who know his faults would reject him and his ministry. The only winner here would be the devil.

Titus 1:6–9

The second list of qualifications for an elder-pastor is found in Titus 1:6–9. Fifteen items are listed, the same number found in 1 Timothy 3. However, the lists do not exactly coincide. Apparently these are not from a standardized list, or they would agree. Of the fifteen in Titus, most are either repeated or are synonyms for the ones in 1 Timothy. There are three notable differences. The prohibition of electing recent converts, as well as the requirement of a good reputation among unbelievers, is omitted, although they may be considered part of the meaning of other requirements. There are also some additions in Titus that are not in 1 Timothy. Only those differences between the lists will be discussed.

General Qualifications

As in 1 Timothy 3:2, one requirement is an umbrella-type word, which includes all the requirements under it. The word *blameless (anegkletos)* is not the same word used in 1 Timothy 3:2 but a synonym. It is actually a stronger word. It literally means "not called in question." It implies "not acquittal merely, but absence so much as of a charge or accusation brought against him." It means not only "unaccusable, but unaccused."[52] In other words, there is not even a hint of impropriety in his character.

Moral and Domestic Qualifications

The first requirement for the office of pastor, "husband of one wife," is also found in 1 Timothy 3:2 (see the discussion on that passage). The second requirement is more specific than 1 Timothy. It says the pastor must have "faithful children." This means, at the very least, that they are believers in Jesus. Children who are pagans would be a tremendous handicap for a pastor-elder. In addition, the pastor's children must not be a source of embarrassment to their father because of unrighteous living. His children should not be guilty of "dissipation or insubordination." *Dissipation* is the Greek word *asotia*, which describes a person who is "wasteful and extravagant and who pours out his substance on personal pleasure."[53]

In Luke 15:13 it is used to describe the "riotous living" of the prodigal son. Its literal meaning is "one who is without salvation." The second word, *insubordination*, describes one who is not in subjection to his father and who is undisciplined.[54] It describes conduct befitting a lost sinner (see 1 Tim. 1:9 and Titus 1:10). In other words, it is not enough for a candidate for the pastoral office to lead his children to Christ; he must disciple them in the way of the Lord. Christianity begins at home. As Barclay says, "All the church service in the world will not atone for the neglect of a man's own family."[55]

Personal Qualifications

The next seven items are related to the candidate's personality. (1) He must not be "self-willed" or "self-pleasing." Kent says this word describes the "headstrong, stubborn man who demands his own way without regard for others."[56] Since a pastor's job is to shepherd and serve the entire flock, there is no room for self-service. He must respect the rights of those he serves. (2) "Not quick-tempered" means not "prone to anger or not soon angry." Barclay says this word, *orgilon*, "is not the anger of the sudden blaze, but the wrath which a man nurses to keep it warm."[57] It is purposely maintained. Such an angry man should not be chosen for this high office. (3–4) "Not given to wine" and "not violent" are exactly the words used in 1 Timothy. (See the previous discussion on 1 Tim. 3:3.)

(5) "Not greedy for money" is *aischrokerde*. This word is found in the qualification for deacons (1 Tim. 3:8). A similar qualification for elders is given in 1 Timothy 3:3. However, a different word, *aphilarguron*, is used there, which means "not a money lover." The phrase in Titus can be interpreted in more than one way. Barclay says it "describes a man who does not care how he makes money."[58] Arndt and Gingrich give its meaning as "fond of dishonest gain."[59] In this context the emphasis is not on getting money by dishonorable dealing, but by using one's position for financial gain. Kelly agrees that this weakness would be a special temptation to those who handled the church's offerings and relief for the poor.[60] (6) *Hospitable* is also listed in 1 Timothy 3:2. (7) The final qualification in this category is "a lover of what is good." This term is very similar to the previous word *hospitable,* which means "a lover of strangers." This word means either a lover of good things or of good people. In this context it probably refers to a man who loves everything that is good. Kent concludes that the overseer "should be an ally and an advocate of everything worthwhile."[61]

Mental Qualification

The same word found in Titus, "sober-minded," has already been considered in 1 Timothy 3:2. It is the Greek word *sophrona*.

Spiritual and Moral Qualifications

The final four requirements fit the moral and spiritual category. The first is the adjective *dikaion*, which means "righteous" or "just." It is a common word in the New Testament; it occurs eighty-one times. There is some question about how it is intended in this passage. It may refer to one's conduct toward others or to a person who lives according to God's laws. Mayer concludes that in this context the term "describes a man who is upright in his dealings with his neighbor and does him no wrong, but these dealings are in accord with the divine standard of right as well."[62]

The second qualification listed is "holy" (*hosion*). This refers to a man's relationship with God. Arndt and Gingrich define it as "devout, pious, pleasing to God, holy."[63] A potential pastor-elder should be one who is pleasing to God because of his sincere reverence for the moral laws of God. A good example would be Joseph who, when tempted by Potiphar's wife, had reverence for the sanctity of marriage and refused to sin against God by violating it (Gen. 39).

A third moral prerequisite is to be "self-controlled" (*egkrate*). This word is an adjective that is formed by combining the preposition *en* (in) with *kratos* (strength or power). Its literal meaning is "having strength within." It came to mean "self-controlled" or "disciplined."[64] There is some overlap here with the fourth qualification in 1 Timothy 2:12. *Sophrona* (sober-minded) also includes the idea of discipline or self-control, but its emphasis is on controlling one's mind or thoughts concerning physical appetites.[65]

The final requirement is that the pastor-elder must be one "holding fast the faithful word." In other words, he must hold firmly to the Word of God. He must cling to it because he recognizes that it is trustworthy. He must not change doctrine but hold on to what he has been taught. Literally the Greek reads, "Clinging to the faithful word according to the teaching (or doctrine)." Mayer is correct when he says that teaching "probably refers to the objective body of Christian truth which is received . . . although its content cannot be delineated, it undoubtedly was that which was taught by Paul himself (cf. Romans 6:17; 16:17), as well as the apostles (cf. 1 Tim. 6:3)."[66]

Two reasons are given for the pastor's "clinging to" the Word. He must be able to teach it in order to "exhort" or encourage the believers. He must be conversant with sound doctrine in order to give the right message. He must also be able to "convict" (refute) those who oppose sound doctrine. To be able to do this the pastor must be schooled in Christian doctrine, understand it, cling to it, and have the ability to teach it (1 Tim. 3:2). Otherwise, the prospective pastor-elder will not be able to fulfill the high purpose of his office.

Conclusion

One might say that it is impossible for anyone to qualify to be a pastor-elder after looking at the qualifications. At the very least one can say the office has extremely high requirements for anyone who wishes to fill it. Few meet the requirements, and none can meet them without the strength given by the indwelling Spirit of God.

Qualifications for a Pastor-Elder

1 Timothy 3:2–7   ## Titus 1:6–9

General Qualification
1. blameless (v. 2)   blameless (v. 6)

Moral Qualification
2. husband of one wife (v. 2)   husband of one wife (v. 6)
                                      just (v. 8)
                                      holy (v. 8)
                                      self-controlled (v. 8)

Mental Qualifications
3. temperate (v. 2)   not self-willed (v. 7)
4. sober-minded (v. 2)   sober-minded (v. 8)
5. of good behavior   (orderly) (v. 2)
6. able to teach (v. 2)   holding fast the faithful word (v. 9)
                                      a lover of what is good (v. 8)

Personal Qualifications
7. hospitable (v. 2)   hospitable (v. 8)
8. not given to wine (v. 3)   not given to wine (v. 7)
9. not violent (v. 3)   not violent (v. 7)
10. gentle (v. 3)
11. not quarrelsome (v. 3)   not quick tempered (v. 8)
12. not covetous (a money-lover) (v. 3)   not greedy for money (v. 7)

Domestic Qualification
13. rules his own house well (v. 4–5)   having faithful children (v. 6)

Christian Experience
14. not a novice (v. 6)

Reputation
15. a good testimony outside the church (v. 7)

A prospective pastor must be one who walks with God and clings to His Word.

Many times men are ordained without careful reference to their moral, spiritual, personal, and doctrinal qualifications. To do this is to degrade the office. The church cannot afford to ignore these guidelines if it is serious about fulfilling its purpose.

5

The Authority of the Pastor-Elder

It has been pointed out in previous chapters that the pastor-elder as shepherd of the flock and overseer of the church has a certain amount of authority in the church. This is an obvious conclusion since he could not carry out his responsibilities effectively if his word had no influence on the congregation. The question is, What kind of authority are pastor-elders given and how far does it extend? A larger question affects the answer to the previous one: Where does authority in the church lie? The obvious answer is that all authority is in Christ, the head of the church. But to whom in the physical world of the church is authority given to govern the church?

Bishop Rule

There are three basic approaches to church government. In the episcopal form of government, authority to rule is given to the bishops *(episkopoi)*.

Examples of this form of government are found in the Anglican, Episcopalian, and Methodist churches. Since it has been demonstrated that pastor, elder, and bishop are all names for one and the same office in the New Testament, there is no biblical basis for making the office of bishop a separate office. The development of this hierarchical structure did not begin to appear until well after the New Testament period. Plummer argues for this approach to church order.[1] He does so on the basis of three brief New Testament references as well as references from second-century church history. The three references are: "Know them that labor among you, and are over you in the Lord, and admonish you" (1 Thess. 5:12–13); "Diotrephes who loves to have the preeminence among them" (3 John 9); and "Obey them that have the rule over you and submit to them" (Heb. 13:17).

From these passages Plummer draws three conclusions. (1) A clear distinction is made between clergy and laity. (2) This is not a temporary arrangement; it is the basis of a permanent organization. (3) A person who has attained the office of elder or bishop holds that position for life.[2] His main argument however is not from Scripture but from church history. He concludes that the authority of the episcopacy has been established and its authority will continue even if it were not established by the apostles.[3]

It is difficult to see how all these conclusions derive from the evidence. It may be agreed that the leaders of the church have authority to lead and the members are exhorted to support them, but this is a big step from a strict division between clergy and laity. It must be concluded that there is little support for this type of church order in Scripture. Its support comes primarily from some later Christian writings. However, other Christian documents do not support bishop rule.[4] At the end of the first century, a church manual, the Didache, taught that each congregation should choose its own bishops and deacons (15:1).

Another important tenet that usually goes with this type of approach is an unbroken succession of bishops from the apostles. As Ryrie points out, however, "There is a legitimate facet to apostolic succession in that the doctrine of the apostles is what all succeeding generations should teach (2 Tim. 22), but that is a succession of doctrine not of ordination."[5]

Elder Rule

A second form of church government is rule by the elders (presbyters—hence it is called "presbyterian"). A distinction is usually made between teaching and ruling elders (1 Tim. 5:17). The teaching elder is the minister or pastor of the congregation. In fact, Mark Brown has concluded, "Presbyterianism stands or falls with the distinction between ruling and teaching elders."[6] The Presbyterian Church in the U.S.A. Constitution clearly defines these as two separate offices. It says:

As he has the oversight of the flock of Christ, he is termed bishop. As he feeds them with spiritual food, he is termed pastor. As he serves Christ in his church, he is termed minister. As it is his duty to be grave and prudent, and an example of the flock, and to govern well in the house and kingdom of Christ, he is termed presbyter or elder. As he is the messenger of God, he is termed the angel of the church.[7]

The office of ruling elder is distinct from the pastoral office in this system. It is described as a second office of elders in the same constitution.

Ruling elders are properly the representatives of the people, chosen by them for the purpose of exercising government and discipline, in conjunction with pastors and ministers. This office has been understood . . . to be designated in the Holy Scriptures, by the title of governments; and of those who rule well, but do not labor in the word and doctrine.[8]

Thus the Presbyterian system has three ordained officers: ministers (teaching elders), ruling elders, and deacons.[9] Like deacons, the ruling elders are selected from among the members of the congregation. It is interesting to note that ministers or teaching elders must have a special calling from God, according to John Calvin. There is no requirement of a special call for ruling elders, nor are any specific spiritual gifts required. According to the majority Presbyterian view, the ruling elder is a layman.[10]

Biblically, there are several problems with this view of church government. First, in the New Testament, qualifications are given for only two offices: pastor-elder-bishop and deacon. No allowances are made for different kinds of elders with different qualifications. There is not one kind that is called of God to pastor and teach and another that is not. Second, the qualifications for all elders, both in 1 Timothy and Titus, is that they must be "able to teach" and defend the congregation against false doctrine. In this system most of the elders do not meet this requirement. Finally, this division into classes of elders is based on only one passing statement in 1 Timothy 5:17, and there is a very real probability that it is based on a misunderstanding of the verse. Those who "rule well" and "those who labor in the word" and doctrine are not two different groups.[11] All elders "rule" (lead) and all elders teach the Word, but not all lead "well" and not all "labor" (toil, work hard) at teaching the Word. This interpretation is supported strongly by the use of the same words in 1 Thessalonians 5:12.

This passage says, "And we urge you, brethren, to recognize those who labor *(kapiao,* work hard) among you, and are over you *(proistemi,* rule, lead) in the Lord and admonish *(noutheteo,* warn, remind) you." All three of the Greek words are participles, and they are all connected with the same article *(the).* This signifies that these three are different functions of the same leaders in the church.[12] It must be that some "rule well" but do not "work hard" at teaching the Word. This underscores again that the primary function of the pastor-elder is teaching the Word. The one who excels at presenting the Word is worthy of "double honor."

There is under the elder-rule system equality between teaching elders, and some insist that this equality includes the ruling elders also. In fact, the debate has been going on for more than a century in Presbyterian circles over the status of the ruling elder. Is he a minister or a layman? Hodge calls it a "new doctrine" that makes all elders to be "bishops, pastors, teachers, and rulers."[13] The two types of elder would be reduced to one office. This would give the ruling elder the same right to preach, ordain, and administer the sacraments. Hodge objected strongly to this view because it is "entirely contrary to the doctrine and practice of all the Reformed Churches."[14] The ruling elder in his view then is a layman who is not specially appointed to preach the gospel. Meyer, on the other hand, argues for the equality of the elders. He says, "Although some groups make the distinction between teaching and ruling elders . . . in the New Testament, the elders engaged in all the functions to a certain extent."[15] He adds that no one leader or elder had any more authority than the others in the local church.

In order to make all elders the same, Meyer has had to come to some other conclusions to be consistent. (1) He concludes that "pastor" is not another title for "elder" in the New Testament; therefore, elders do not have to have this gift (called pastor-teacher) or any other spiritual gift in order to perform their ministry effectively, though some probably did have gifts related to the elder role.[16] Others in the congregation may have the gift of pastor, but they need not be elders. (2) Calvin believed in a special call for ministers or teaching elders. However, this cannot be required if all elders are to be completely equal. Anyone can aspire to this ministry as long as the qualifications are met.[17]

The question should be asked, "What part does God play in all of this?" Does ministry involve the exercise of spiritual gifts to be effective? Or can a person serve God with his natural ability alone? It is true that some ministries can be performed by those who do not have special gifts. Timothy is told to "do the work of an evangelist" (2 Tim. 4:5), though he was not an evangelist as such. On the other hand, what are spiritual gifts for anyway if believers can operate just as well without them? The obvious answer is, They cannot do by natural ability what the Spirit can do through them by spiritual gifts. Three times the gift of teaching is connected with the office of pastor-elder as an integral part of the ministry of that office, and the office cannot be separated from the ministry (Eph. 4:11; 1 Tim. 3:2; Titus 1:9). Walvoord defines this gift as "a supernatural ability to explain and apply the truths which had been already received by the church."[18] This gift does not presuppose a superior knowledge of the truth but an understanding of it and an ability to explain it to others in such a way that they can grasp it.

All elders, like pastor-elders, lead and govern in the life of the church. However, there is no requirement of a gift of "leadership" or "administration" mentioned in 1 Timothy or Titus beyond the ability to "lead" or "govern" one's own household well. This would require at least some natural ability in the area of leadership, but it is not connected with a spiritual gift such as teaching.

Congregational Rule

The congregational form of government means that ultimate authority for governing the church resides in the members jointly. This authority comes from Christ who is the head of the body, and the entire body administers the church according to the patterns given in Scripture. There are only two offices in the church, pastors (elders) and deacons. Ordination to the office of pastor does not carry any special gift of grace to minister, but it is a recognition of God's call to the office. Congregationalism also means that each local church is an autonomous unit with no organization over it except Christ the Head. This does not mean that the entire congregation must vote on every decision. Responsibilities may be delegated to leaders or any other member of the church, and every member, including pastors and deacons, has the same vote.

The democratic structure of congregational government is supported by a number of New Testament principles.

1. Church Discipline

Jesus said if a brother sins against you, go to him. If he will not hear you, take one or two people with you. If he still refuses to hear you, bring the matter before the church (Matt. 18:15–17). In other words, the final court of appeal in matters of discipline is the church as a whole, not the officers or any representative body. This pattern was practiced by the church at Corinth under Paul's direction. The apostles say, "In the name of our Lord Jesus Christ, when you are gathered together, along with my spirit, with the power of our Lord Jesus Christ, deliver such a one to

Satan for the destruction of the flesh" (1 Cor. 5:4–5). Concerning this same man Paul speaks of the church's action in disciplining him. He says, "This punishment which was inflicted by the majority is sufficient for such a man" (2 Cor. 2:6). Two facts stand out in this incident as far as the practice of discipline is concerned. First, Paul instructed them to act when the whole church was assembled. Then, he says the action was taken by the majority, which suggests a vote on the matter or at least some polling of the opinion of the entire church. Paul also commands the Thessalonian church to withdraw from any brother who is guilty of "disorderly" conduct (2 Thess. 3:6, 14–15). This instruction is given to the church as a whole.

2. Elections of Officers

Beginning in Acts 1, before the official inauguration of the church at Pentecost, the 120 disciples who made up the first church under the leadership of Peter nominated the two candidates to fill the place vacated by Judas. Luke says that "they proposed two: Joseph called Barsabas, who was surnamed Justus, and Matthias." The entire group took part in the selection process.

The first deacons were also selected by the congregation. Under the leadership of the apostles, they were called together and asked to "seek out from among you seven men of good reputation, full of the Holy Spirit and wisdom, whom we may appoint over this business" (Acts 6:3). It is clear that the apostles led the church to make this decision, but it is also clear that what they proposed "pleased the whole multitude." The whole church approved the apostles' suggestion. As a result the church chose Stephen, Philip, and five others, and brought them to the apostles. After prayer and the laying on of hands, these first deacons began their ministry. Several things are evident from this account. (1) The leadership of the apostles was respected by the church as a whole. There was a tremendous display of unity that demonstrates both the leadership ability of the apostles and the spiritual commitment of the believers to follow godly leadership. (2) The apostles trusted the rest of the believers to choose the first deacons according to the qualifications laid down. They did not feel it necessary to oversee the entire process but went about their other ministries. The whole point of giving the qualifications for elders in 1 Timothy 3 and Titus 1 was so the church could choose qualified men for this position.

Against this view some may argue that in Acts 14:23 Paul and Barnabas "appointed elders in every church." However, even if "they" refers to Paul and Barnabas alone (not including the other believers), this does not necessarily mean that they took this action without any assistance from the local believers. In fact, the process is not detailed at all. It is not likely that they governed by fiat since that was not Paul's approach in other matters. To Philemon, for example, he says, "Though I might be very bold in Christ to command you what is fitting, yet for love's sake I rather appeal to you" (v. 8–9). The example of Peter and the other apostles was to seek the agreement of the whole church. There is no compelling reason to believe that their approach was any different in Acts 14. Neither is it different in Titus 1:5, where Paul instructs Titus to get things organized and "appoint elders in every city." Again, the entire process is not described, but one thing is sure: It would have been a lot more difficult for Titus to appoint elders without the consent of the people than it would for Paul himself to do so.

3. Election of Representatives and Approving of Missionaries

When Paul was getting ready to take an offering from the churches of Macedonia to aid the believers at Jerusalem, he sent instructions to Corinth concerning the collection (1 Cor. 16:4). In those instructions he says to the church, "Whomever you approve by your letters I will send to bear your gift to Jerusalem." It was left to the church to choose those who would represent them in this matter.

In a similar matter, when Paul and Barnabas were called by the Holy Spirit to go out on the first missionary journey, the matter was brought before the entire church. It was not that the church had veto power over the Holy Spirit's call to these men, but they "fasted and prayed" over the matter. They seriously sought God's will, and when they were satisfied that God was indeed in this call, they gave them their blessing to go out from their church. They did this symbolically by laying hands on them. The fact that Saul and Barnabas felt some responsibility to the church that "sent them" is demonstrated upon their return to Antioch. They "gathered the church together" and "reported all that God had done with them" (Acts 14:27). Again, he returned to Antioch and spent some time there after the second missionary journey (Acts 18:22–23).

4. Spiritual Gifts in the Body

The New Testament teaches clearly that all believers have at least one spiritual gift. Paul says in 1 Corinthians 12:7, "But the manifestation of the Spirit is given to each one for the profit of all." Again he says, "But one and the same Spirit works all these things distributing to each one individually as He wills" (v. 11). The illustration is that the church is like a body with many members, and all are necessary for it to function properly (1 Cor. 12:12, 21–27; Rom. 12:4–5). All of the members have "been made to drink into one Spirit" (1 Cor. 12:13). The implication is that all members have some responsibility in the ministry of the church. Since all have the Spirit and all have some responsibility placed on them because of the impartation of a spiritual gift, then all are capable of having a voice in the affairs of the church. Since all have gifts and no one has all of the gifts (1 Cor. 12:29–30), it is probable that there will be people in the congregation who have abilities for ministry that the pastors and deacons do not have. It is the job of the leaders to oversee these ministries, but no one is more important or less important to the body because of the gift he has or doesn't have. No one has any gift because he deserves it. They are "grace gifts" given to each one according to God's will and not because of anyone's merit.

5. Saints Judging Personal and Doctrinal Disputes

One of the problems in the Corinthian church was that members were taking fellow believers to court before pagan judges for the whole pagan world to see. Paul reminds them that the saints will judge both the world and the angels (1 Cor. 6:2–3). If this be the case, saints are capable of judging the things of this life. In fact, these matters are small by comparison. The important point for this discussion is found in verse 4. When you have disputes pertaining to this physical life, then "appoint [seat as judges] those who are least esteemed in the church to judge."[19] Any believer can judge between brethren better than a pagan judge. If then all believers are qualified to judge temporal matters, why are they not qualified to have a voice in the government of the church?

Someone might argue this does not mean they are qualified to judge doctrinal matters. Let us consider that point for a moment. Paul says to those who are prophets, "Let two or three prophets speak, and let the others judge" (1 Cor. 14:29). Who are these prophets? It is clear that they are not all pastor-elders. This is evidenced by the fact that some women prophesied (1 Cor. 11:4). Philip the deacon had four daughters who prophesied. They were not forbidden to do so as long as they did so in a proper manner (v. 5–6). Prophets also had the responsibility to judge the prophecy of other prophets. This must have been for the purpose of assuring the church that each message was truly in line with the spirit and teaching of the Lord. They could not do this without judging doctrinal matters.

Someone might also argue that this is not relevant for today because prophecy has ceased and therefore prophets are no longer needed to judge. This is a debatable point, but regardless of the answer to this issue, other New Testament data must be considered. After Paul and Barnabas's first missionary journey, a dispute arose in the Antioch church over the requirements for salvation, especially that of Gentiles. A delegation was sent to Jerusalem over the matter, and the so-called Jerusalem Conference was held (Acts 15). The delegation from Antioch was received by the church, including the apostles and elders. Verse 6 implies that they met privately with the apostles and elders to discuss the problem. (Gal. 2:2 supports the idea of a private meeting with the apostles.) It seems, however, that after much debate, the matter was presented to the whole congregation (v. 12). James the brother of Jesus proposed a solution to the debate which supported the theology of Paul and Barnabas (v. 13ff.). The letter that James wrote to inform the churches of their decision on this matter was supported by the "whole church" (v. 22). Judas and Silas were chosen from the Jerusalem church to go with Paul and Barnabas to deliver the letter from James. This is the same Silas who accompanied Paul on his second missionary journey.

Another instance of the entire congregation's involvement in the affairs of the church is recorded in Acts 21:22. In this instance Paul had returned from his third missionary journey. Accusations had circulated that Paul was teaching Jews to forsake Jewish customs such as circumcision (v. 21). James, who was still the leader of the church at that time, made this statement: "The assembly must certainly meet." A plan that included the taking of a vow by Paul was devised by James, apparently to assure the congregation that Paul was not guilty of the accusations. What transpired at the meeting is not recorded, but it seems that the congregation was in agreement with the plan.

6. Priesthood of All Believers

Peter says concerning the church, "You also, as living stones, are being built up a spiritual house, a holy priesthood, to offer up spiritual sacrifices acceptable to God through Jesus Christ" (1 Pet. 2:5). Again he says, "But you are a chosen generation, a royal priesthood, a holy nation, his own special people" (2:9). The task of a priest involves representing the people before God, but the New Testament makes clear that there is only "one Mediator between God and men, the Man Christ Jesus" (1 Tim. 2:5). In the Old Testament, priests did for the people what they could not do for themselves. They offered various kinds of sacrifices for the people. In the New Testament, the believer has "boldness to enter the Holiest by the blood of Jesus" (Heb. 10:19).

No priest is needed to offer sacrifice because atonement has already been made by Jesus Himself once for all. No priest is required to present requests to God because every believer has the right to enter the "holiest place," the presence of God, to make his requests "known to God" (Phil. 4:6). The pastor-elder is not then a priest. He may perform the priestly duty of praying for the congregation, but this is the duty of all believers, not just the pastor. Paul says to Timothy, "I desire therefore that the men pray everywhere, lifting up holy hands, without wrath and doubting" (1 Tim. 2:8). To the Thessalonians he says, "Pray without ceasing" (5:17). Many other passages could be cited to support the necessity of all believers to be fervent in prayer (see 2 Cor. 1:11; 9:14; Phil. 1:19; 4:6; Col. 4:2; and James 5:16).

Since believers are qualified to come to God directly without the aid of a mediator, and since they are all indwelt by the Holy Spirit (1 Cor. 12:13), which makes them capable of understanding God's Word (John 11:13), why should not every believer who is in right fellowship with God be able to have a voice in the business of the church? All believers are equal and responsible before God. Authority comes from the Head of the church, Christ. All believers are charged with the responsibility of carrying out the commands of Christ, including the Great Commission (Matt. 28:19–20). The command to evangelize the whole world and disciple all believers is given not only to the apostles or elders but to every believer. Since all are responsible before God to pray, to witness, to disciple, all should have a part in approving the direction of the ministry. The difference between the pastor-elder and the rest is that he is the overseer of the work, but all should be engaged in the work.

Pastoral Authority

What kind of authority does the pastor have to lead a congregation? If all believers are equal before God and Christ is the Head of the church, what difference is there between the pastor's role and the role of others in the church? In the New Testament there is a tension between the pastor's role as bishop or overseer of the congregation on one hand and the equality of all believers on the other.

The Leadership Factor

The title *pastor* refers to a "shepherd" of sheep. Believers are referred to as sheep on several occasions in the New Testament (see John 10; 21:12–17; 1 Pet. 2:25 for examples). If one takes this analogy as having any descriptive value at all, it is clear that the shepherd is not told how to do his job by the sheep. He is to take care of the sheep, feed them, and protect them. Their responsibility is to follow the shepherd. Three times the writer of Hebrews admonishes his readers to follow their leaders. Hebrews 13:17 says, "Obey those who have the rule over you, and be submissive, for they watch for your souls." The Hebrews are also told to "remember" their leaders and to "greet" them. *Keep them in mind* (Heb. 13:7, *mnemoneuo*) does not mean simply to remember who they are but to remember both that they are the leaders appointed by God and that the church must cooperate with them. "To greet" (Heb. 13:24, *aspazomai*) means to "welcome" or "salute." It can also mean "to pay respect to," or to "wish someone well."[20] The church should have a proper attitude toward its leaders, recognizing that the leaders have its interests at heart. The point is that shepherds not only take care of but lead the sheep.

The New Testament pastor-elder is also called an "overseer" (bishop) of the church. An overseer is a supervisor over the work. A lot of ministries should go on in the church that cannot be done by the pastor. Members have gifts that the pastor does not and thus the responsibility to serve in ways the pastor cannot. It is not the responsibility of the pastor-elder to do everything but to oversee the ministry. "He must see that the work is done and done properly. For this he must give account" (Heb. 13:17).

One of the qualifications of a pastor-elder is that he "rules [leads] his own house well" (1 Tim. 3:4). There is no requirement of a special gift of leadership or administration to be a pastor, but some proficiency in leadership is necessary. He is the one who "stands in front" *(proistamenon,* see Rom. 12:8). He is the one who sees to it that the ship is on course (1 Cor. 12:28). He is to govern or administrate in the church in the same manner that he would in his own family.

Not only does the pastor-elder have the authority of the shepherd and protector of the flock, as well as the overseer and leader of the congregation, but he is also the primary teacher of the church. In effect, this makes the entire congregation his disciples. Under Christ they are to learn from him. The Word of God has authority inherently. One who knows and expounds the Scriptures wields a powerful spiritual weapon. One cannot use it without unleashing the power of God (1 Cor. 1:18). It is imperative, then, that a good pastor be a vibrant, growing believer himself, because he cannot teach what he does not know. He cannot lead where he has not been. He must feed the flock of God. His authority does not come by virtue of his office, although the congregation should respect anyone who holds the office; his authority comes through the performance of his ministry to them.

Finally, he has the authority of the call. Pastors are pastors because they are chosen and sent by God, or at least they should be. If God has gifted a man for the pastoral ministry and placed him in it, then the authority needed to carry out that ministry is also given by the one who called him. The only warning is that a pastor must be sure he is carrying out God's will and not his own.

The Equality Factor

The other side of the equation is the equality of all believers before God. About this Emil Brunner writes, "These are indeed persons to whom an official duty has been allocated, the episcopoi . . . But this differentiation of the gifts of grace [charismata] does not create any differences in jurisdiction or rank."[21] Pastor-elders are instructed in the New Testament concerning how they are to rule (lead) the church. First, they are instructed not to attempt to become "lords over those entrusted" to their care (1 Pet. 5:3). The pastor should not try to "subdue" the congregation in order to "gain power over" them.[22] On the contrary, the pastor is to be an example to the flock. This is the same admonition Jesus gave to anyone who wanted to be a leader among the believers (Matt. 20:26). It should not be in the church as it is in the world, where leaders love to exercise their authority. Christian leaders should become servants.

A necessary ingredient for servanthood is humility. The great example of humility is Jesus Himself. He not only taught it; He displayed it. He humbled Himself and "became obedient to the point of death" (Phil. 2:8).

Another example is the apostle Paul. We do not ourselves preach but Christ, Paul said (2 Cor. 4:5). To make sure Paul did not exalt himself, God gave him a "thorn in the flesh" so that he would not trust in his own strength but rest in Him. Paul realized that his weakness allowed the "power of Christ to rest" upon him (2 Cor. 12:9–10). Paul's display of servanthood was misunderstood by some. They saw it as weakness or even cowardice (2 Cor. 10:7–11). But as Strauch says, "Humility is not a symptom of weakness or incompetence, but of true self-understanding, godly wisdom, and self-control."[23]

Speaking of the church, Brunner says that in the body of Christ there is no caste system; "even the men of the Spirit do not constitute for Paul a spiritual aristocracy."[24] There is no hierarchy in the body of Christ. All the members have equal value before God. They must work together to make the body function in a manner that glorifies God. As it has been pointed out, all believers have spiritual gifts that are necessary for the body to function completely. All believers are priests who have full access to God Himself. With all this in mind, how does one reconcile the factors of leadership and equality?

A Synthesis

On one hand the pastor-elder is a shepherd who is in charge of the sheep. He is an overseer of all the ministry of the church. He is to see to it that all of the needs of the members receive ministry. He is to lead the sheep because they are not independent travelers who do well on their own. They need protection from false teachers who seem to be at work constantly to lead them astray. They need a pastor to teach them and remind them constantly of the right ways of the Lord. They are sheep.

On the other hand, all believers are fellow servants of God who are to serve one another (Gal. 5:13). They are not only to be servants of righteousness (Rom. 6:18–19), but they each have gifts to make them more effective in their service. Add to this the fact that all members are equal and responsible before God and that all authority comes from Christ. No mediator is necessary, for all believers are priests unto Him. Jesus said, "For where two or three are gathered together in My name, I am there in the midst of them" (Matt. 18:20).

This is what makes the pastor's job so difficult. He must lead and preside over a group of believer-priest sheep. The positive side is that they have great potential to be used of God if led properly. The other side of the issue is that they have great potential for mischief and for going astray. That is precisely why God appointed pastors in the church, not to lord it over them, but to lead them to maturity in Christ.

Practical Application

In today's church are many voices trying to tell pastors and churches how to succeed in their ministry. Some say that in order to have a growing church, strong leadership is required. Most writers on pastoral leadership insist that a CEO style of leadership is anathema to successful pastoral leadership. However, when one considers what is being said, some seem to take the CEO position. Peter Wagner, in his book *Leading Your Church to Growth,* advocates a strong managerial stance on the part of the pastor who wants his church to be more mission-oriented.[25] He quotes W. R. Douglas as saying, "The pastor at a growing church needs to be high on task orientation and low on relationship orientation."[26] He seems to support a controlling type of leadership. Bob Dale lists the "commander" style as an efficient style of church leadership. Although he favors what he calls the "catalyst" style, he does not dismiss the commander style as inappropriate to the needs of the church.[27]

Many other books discuss this type of approach. The *Issachar Factor,* by Martin and McIntosh, advocates strong authoritative leadership from the pastoral staff, especially the senior pastor. Pastors are to lead the church, generate the vision, and mobilize the congregation.[28] Pastoral care is relegated to small groups. This ministry should be delegated to well-trained laypeople. The pastor is then free to dream, develop strategies, and organize.[29] These strategies are based on his research into the current trends of church growth. Norman Sawchuck supports the same conclusions. He observes that a "task-oriented" leader is not going to be a strong shepherd but will be a strong CEO.[30]

It is true that the larger a congregation becomes, the more organizational skill will be needed to keep it on track. The question must be asked, however, "Is it proper to refer to a pastor-elder as a chief operating officer? Or is that term a business term that is out of place in the church?" When the church in Jerusalem began to grow rapidly after Pentecost, more leaders were needed to minister to the church. But apostles did not spend more of their time studying business and marketing strategies; they gave themselves "to prayer and the ministry of the Word" (Acts 6:4). This is not to say that everything that is taught under the heading of church growth is wrong but that it must be measured by the Word. The question must be asked, "Are we following the dictates of Scripture or being pragmatic—doing whatever seems to work for the moment?" Pragmatism is like some medicines. It may make you feel better temporarily, but it could have disastrous side effects down the line. A case in point is the Willow Creek seeker-service movement. Some of the long-range problems that have resulted from this way of "doing church" are now becoming apparent.[31]

Just because something is successful in bringing numbers of people to church does not mean it will succeed in making them committed disciples of Jesus. If it does not teach the Word of God systematically and in depth, it will ultimately fail because it does not fulfill the second half of the Great Commission (Matt. 28:20). The only way a Christian can grow spiritually is by consuming the "milk of God's Word" (1 Pet. 2:2). Jesus said that the church is to teach all that He commanded, not just the part that is popular. Otherwise, the result will be a shallow, immature church that does not understand its own mission.

At the other end of the spectrum are those who talk about the servant-leader concept to describe what a pastor should be.[32] This is a good description, if it is followed. Practically speaking, this balance is difficult to maintain. Especially in the smaller church setting, the pastor's job is to serve the congregation. He serves as a chaplain to the group but is not expected, or in many cases allowed, to be the leader of the church. Pastors tend to stay only a short time, eighteen months to two years in smaller churches; therefore, the pastor leaves before he assumes any real position of leadership in the group. Often he is forced to leave by the leadership because he is beginning to take the place of the leader of the church. Because of low pay and high service demands (visiting the sick, etc.), little time is spent in the main business of growing disciples in the church—prayer and the ministry of the Word. Because of this, members either seek Bible teaching elsewhere, or they do not grow at all.

What is the solution to the problem? The solution is to get back to the pattern found in the New Testament. Pastors need to understand that their first task is to teach people the right ways of the Lord, both by word and by example. Congregations need to understand that the pastor serves them first by feeding them with the Word of the Lord. This does not exclude other kinds of ministry, but without this one the other ministries have no content.

Conclusion

Of the different approaches to church government, the congregational form has the most support in Scripture. Under this type of government, the pastor-elder is the leader of the church, but ultimate authority to determine the direction of the church is given by Christ to the congregation as a whole. This is demonstrated by the choosing of leaders and representatives by the church and by the discipling of members. Equality of members of the body also supports this conclusion. Equality is demonstrated by the giving of the Holy Spirit and spiritual gifts to all believers and by the priesthood of all believers.

The pastor-elder's authority comes not because of his superiority in any way, but because he is called by God and given the responsibility by the Lord to take care of God's flock. He has the authority of one commissioned by God to deliver His message. He leads by virtue of his call, his message, and his righteous example. He is the shepherd of a flock of sheep, but they are not ordinary sheep. They are believer-priest sheep.

The Pastor-Elder and the Deacon

There is general agreement that the churches of the New Testament had two types of ministers: pastor-elders, who gave general oversight to the ministry of the church, and deacons, who gave a ministry of service to the poor and needy. The office of deacon was first established in the Jerusalem church in response to the growing needs of the congregation (Acts 6:1–6). Although the seven officers chosen were not called "deacons" (*diakonos*), the job for which they were chosen was "to deacon" (*diakonein*).

A problem arose concerning the providing of food to the Greek-speaking widows, who reported that they had been neglected in the "daily distribution" (*diakonia*). The apostles called a church meeting to discuss the problem. They did not believe it was right for them to spend their time dealing with this question because it would take away from their spiritual ministry to the congregation. The church agreed, and seven were appointed to take care of this "business." Though they were not at first called deacons, their first task was "to serve *[diakonein]* tables" (Acts 6:2).

The Meaning of the Word *Deacon*

Thayer lists three meanings for the word *diakonos*. (1) It refers to one who executes the commands of another such as a master. Such a one is a servant, attendant, or minister. (2) In the church it refers to one who cares for the poor and has charge of and distributes the money allotted for them. (3) It can refer to a waiter, one who serves food and drink.[1]

All of the New Testament uses of *diakonos* fall into two categories. First, there is the general or generic use of *deacon,* which means a servant or minister. In addition, there is the official use, which refers to an officer of the church. The term is used thirty times in the New Testament. Of these, all but three are used generically to refer to a servant rather than an official. Jesus said that "whoever desires to become great among you should be your servant" (*diakonos,* Matt. 20:26).[2] The king's servants (Matt. 22:13) and the servants at Cana of Galilee (John 2:5a) are referred to as deacons.

A number of people are referred to as deacons (servants) who obviously did not hold the official title or office of deacon. Jesus refers to all of His followers as *diakonos* and promises that they will be where He is (John 12:26). The civil authorities are spoken of as "God's ministers" (deacons). Jesus Himself is called a "servant [deacon] to the circumcision for the truth of God" (Rom. 15:8). Phoebe is called a "servant of the church" (Rom. 16:1). Paul and Apollos are "ministers [deacons] through whom you believed" (1 Cor. 3:5). Paul is also called a "minister of the new covenant" (2 Cor. 3:6), one of the "ministers of God" (2 Cor. 6:4), and a "minister [deacon] of the gospel" (Eph. 3:7; Col. 1:23, 25). Tychicus is called a "faithful minister [deacon] in the Lord" (Eph. 6:21; Col. 4:7). Epaphrus is referred to as "a faithful minister of Christ on your behalf" (Col. 1:7). Timothy is also called a "minister [deacon] and fellow-laborer in the gospel" (1 Thess. 3:2). Paul exhorts Timothy to "be a good minister [deacon] of Jesus Christ" (1 Tim. 4:6).

Not only are these faithful servants called deacons, but there is a warning that Satan will try to mislead the church by sending false ministers. Satan's "ministers [deacons]" will "transform themselves into ministers of righteousness" (2 Cor. 11:15). *Diakonos* is used only three times in the official sense. It appears in Philippians 1:1, where Paul addresses his letter to all the saints in Philippi "with the bishops and deacons." In addition, it occurs twice in the list of qualifications for the office of deacon (1 Tim. 3:8, 12).

About the concept of "office," Edward Schweizer writes:

> As a general term for what we call "office,"
> namely the service of individuals within the church,
> there is, with a few exceptions, only one word:
> diakonia. Thus the New Testament throughout and
> uniformly chooses a word that is entirely unbiblical
> and nonreligious and never includes association
> with a particular dignity or position. . . . The verb
> . . . denotes in Philo and Josephus waiting at table
> and serving in general . . . diakonos means the
> servant of the prophet.[3]

In view of the other terms available, it is conspicuous that this term was chosen rather than a word like *archon,* ruler, or *arche,* head, which would emphasize authority in the church. Neither was a word like *leitourgos,* which might have had the connotation of religious or priestly service. The only connotation for *diakonos* is servant.

There is no such office as deacon in Judaism, but Moulton and Milligan conclude that there is "now abundant evidence that the way had been prepared for the Christian usage of this word by its technical application to the holders of various offices within pagan religions of the first century before Christ."[4] These references support the conclusion that the position of deacon is an official office. An official position implies a certain amount of authority in the church, and without a doubt *ministry* and *authority* seem to be somewhat contradictory terms. However, Schweizer is correct when he says that "the deacon's authority does not rest on the ground of position or dignity, but on obedience that is given because a person is overcome by the ministry that is performed."[5] His authority comes through service.

Qualifications for the Office

There is still some debate over the question of whether the appointment of the seven to serve tables (Acts 6:1–6) marks the beginning of this office. It has been pointed out that even though they are not given the title *deacons,* they are told "to deacon" (wait on tables). Saucy observes that Luke gives this account a prominent position, which suggests the creation of a new office.[6] If these are not deacons, then that leaves us with these two questions: (1) When did the office begin if this was not the beginning? (2) What happened to this unnamed office? Was it a temporary one that faded with time?

Although the qualifications are not exactly the same, they are parallel to those listed in 1 Timothy 3:8–13. The best answer is that this was the beginning of the office, and the spiritual and practical qualifications given here were expounded upon by Paul in 1 Timothy 3.

The three qualifications given here are: (1) good reputation, (2) full of the Holy Spirit, and (3) full of wisdom (Acts 6:3). The word for "good reputation" is *martureo,* which could also mean to have a good "testimony" or a good "witness."[7] The second qualification is that one must show "all the marks of the work of the Holy Spirit" in his life.[8] There is a difference between "being filled with the Spirit" and being "full of the Spirit." "Being filled" refers to a momentary situation. That person is under the control of the Spirit at this time.[9] *Full* is an adjective that describes a characteristic of that person. It can be said that a general characteristic of such a person is that he is "full of the Holy Spirit." His life is generally under the control of the Spirit of God. The final characteristic is wisdom. The deacons should be known for their practical wisdom, which would enable them to properly manage the money contributed for the needy.

First Timothy 3:8–13 offers a more complete account of the requirements to serve as a deacon. The fact that these are given along with the qualifications for the overseers shows the close association between the deacons and the pastor-elders. These will be divided into several headings. They are very similar to those of the pastor-elder.

Personal Character

In the first place, the deacon should be "reverent" or "serious." These adjectives cover both the inward attitude and the outward conduct of the deacon. Lea and Griffin point out, "The term combines such ideas as dignity, earnestness of purpose, and winsome attractiveness."[10] He should be one who is worthy of respect.

Next, the deacon should not be "double-tongued." He should not be one who gives out conflicting stories among the congregation. He should be one who is consistent in what he says. Since in his ministry he has constant contact with members of the church, he can cause great problems in the church if he has a loose tongue.

"Not given to much wine" is a little different from the "not given to wine" requirement for pastor-elders. The deacon is not one who "lingers beside his wine." Hendrickson says, "The qualified deacon is moderate in his use of wine if he drinks any."[11] It is clear that wine was the common beverage in the first-century Mediterranean world. It was mixed with water in order to purify the water and make the wine last longer.[12] However, the deacon must be known for his sobriety. Kent is correct when he says that this "does not mean that Christians today can use liquor in moderate amounts. The wine employed for the common beverage was very largely water. The social stigma and the tremendous social evils that accompany drinking today did not attach themselves to the use of wine as the common beverage in the homes of Paul's day."[13]

The final personal qualification is to be "not greedy for money." This qualification is similar to that of the elder in verse 3, "not a money lover." This word, *aischrokerdeis,* means "fond of dishonest gain."[14] Since the office of deacon involves the handling and distribution of money for the needy, there is temptation and opportunity for embezzlement of these funds. Therefore, the deacon should be one who is scrupulously honest and not at all greedy. Erdman has reminded us, "Judas was not the last treasurer who betrayed his Lord for a few pieces of silver."[15]

Spiritual Life

The deacon is not required to have the gift of teaching; however, he does need to have a strong grip on the "mystery of the faith." The term *mystery* as used by Paul refers to "something hidden but now revealed." The deep truths of the faith are now an "open secret."[16] "The faith" is the

Christian faith, and it is here "regarded as an objective body of teaching."[17] These truths have been made known to believers by divine revelation, not by man's searching for them. The deacon should have a good understanding of the mysteries of God's Word and be confirmed in them. Especially, he should understand the mystery of Christ who is the center of God's redemptive plan (Col. 4:3). Kelly expands "the mystery of the faith" to include "the totality of hidden truths" or "the key articles of the Christian kerygma or creed."[18]

The job of the deacon is to bring spiritual comfort and ministry to others. Therefore, he cannot just hold the truths of God's Word as abstract beliefs that are not connected to his lifestyle, but he must hold them with a "pure conscience." His life must be above reproach. For his conscience to be pure, his life must be pure. Someone has said that a pure conscience is the jewelry box in which the treasure of the mystery is to be kept.

Christian Experience

Candidates for the office of deacon, like the pastor-elders, should be tested before they serve. The verb *tested* is in the present tense, which indicates that the testing involved is not a formal test like an exam that one must pass but a period of continual observation or testing to prove one is qualified. A period of time would be required to ascertain whether the candidate is indeed qualified. Like the pastor-elder, he should not be a recent convert (newly planted). Once the candidate has been examined and there is no cause for accusation against him (blameless), he is ready to serve.

Morality

The same standard applies for deacons that is required of pastor-elders. They are to be "husbands of one wife." This means they are not divorced or accused of any other marital unfaithfulness. (See the previous discussion on the qualifications for pastor-elders in 1 Tim. 3:2.)

Domestic Relations

Part of the testing of deacons must include their family life. As in the case of the pastor-elders, they must "rule [lead] their children and their own houses well." They must have the respect of their family and have the ability to manage the affairs of the household well. Kent is correct when he observes, "This requirement in the case of a deacon is probably not so much to demonstrate ability in rulership as it is an evidence of Christian character."[19]

A Qualified Wife

Verse 11 contains a puzzle which cannot be solved to everyone's satisfaction. The Greek text can be translated two different ways. The King James Version, New King James Version, English Standard Version, and the New International Version translate the word *gunaikos* as "wives." This would take the verse to mean that a deacon must have a qualified wife. Other translations such as the New American Standard Bible, the Revised Standard Version, Jerusalem Bible, New American Bible, and the Holman Christian Standard Bible read simply "the woman." The question is, which women? There are two translations and at least three opinions concerning the application of this verse.

The first option is to apply these requirements to the wives of deacons. The best argument for this view is that the context before verse 11 and after verse 11 definitely describes the qualifications of deacons. Why would something totally different be buried in the middle of a discussion of deacon qualifications if it is not part of the requirements for deacons? Some argue that the word *likewise*, which introduces the verse, indicates a different group of persons is being described. The different class or group could well be deacons' wives.

Against this view is the fact that there is no pronoun or article to make it definitely refer to "wives" instead of to other women in the church. The objection is also raised, Why would there be requirements for deacons' wives when no requirements are given for the wives of pastor-elders. This last objection can be explained by the nature of the deacons' ministry. Since they were in charge of taking care of widows, their wives would be very important in helping them with this ministry to women.

A second view is that verse 11 is speaking of women deacons. Supporting this view is the fact that the term *diakanos* can apply to women. Phoebe is called a deacon in Romans 16:1. However, it is not clear that the word is used in its official sense. It may only mean that she was a servant of the church. It is suggested by some that verses 8–10 are general qualifications for deacons/deaconesses. Specific qualifications for deaconesses are given in verse 11. The reason the title *women* is used is that there was no specific title for female deacons. Then, in verses 12 and 13, the specific qualifications for male deacons are given.[20]

This view is doubtful for two reasons. (1) The use of the term *likewise* in 3:11 makes clear that the author is referring to a different group, not to part of the deacons. (2) The author refers back to deacons in 3:12–13. It is clear that the deacons addressed in these verses are men.

Since they do not have the same qualifications, they must not be of the same office.

Verse 11 speaks to a group of women who were engaged in the same types of service as the deacons. Since they are not given a title, it is unclear whether they are the wives of deacons or other women in the church. Hultgren says, "Perhaps the best that we can conclude is that while diakonos applies to male deacons, there were also women [not 'wives'] involved in diakonal service, even if they do not bear the title in this community."[21] Fairbairn suggests the possibility that the passage is deliberately vague so as to allow the inclusion of both the deacons' wives and other qualified women.[22] It is obvious that women were needed to perform the kind of work assigned to deacons because of the nature of first-century society. He says:

> And considering the greater separation which then existed between the sexes, and the extreme jealousy which guarded the approaches to female society, it was in a manner indispensable that women, with some sort of delegated authority, should often be entrusted with various kinds of diakonal service.[23]

The relationship of the women mentioned in verse 11 and the widows (1 Tim. 5:9ff.) is very obscure. There is no explanation of it anywhere in Scripture. An order of women deacons did arise in the primitive church of the third and fourth centuries. They assisted with the baptism of women and ministered to the poor and the sick, especially in homes where the husband was not a believer.[24]

There were four requirements for these "women" who served. First, they must be "reverent" (semnas). This is the same requirement mentioned in verse 8 for deacons, which also indicates this is a different group than deacons;

otherwise, the same requirement would not appear twice. The second qualification is that the woman must not be a "slanderer." The word used is *diabolos,* one who spreads malicious gossip. One must resist the temptation to repeat things that are discovered in the course of ministry. This can be devastating to the church and to all who are concerned.

The third qualification is that the women must be "temperate." This is the same term used of the pastor-elder in 1 Timothy 3:2. The literal meaning of *nephalious* is sober or temperate in the use of wine. Its expanded meaning may include sober in judgment or free from any kind of excess.

Finally, the "women" who serve must be "faithful in all things." The word *pistos* means "trustworthy, faithful, dependable, inspiring trust or faith."[25] All things are included in this requirement, but the woman should surely be trustworthy and dependable in her duties relating to ministry. Above that, she should be faithful to her husband and family, to the Lord Jesus, and to the church.

The Role of the Deacon

The exact nature and duties of the New Testament deacon are not systematically described anywhere in Scripture. The origin of the office is still being debated; however, the traditional view is that it had its beginning in the appointment of the seven (Acts 6), although they are not specifically called deacons.[26] This view is widely held because the seven were elected to serve *(diakoneo)* tables (6:3), and were instructed to serve as deacons (1 Tim. 3:10, *diakoneo).* Their ministry was intended to aid the apostles by taking care of some of the physical needs of the congregation. Otherwise the apostles would have to "lay down the word of God" in order to serve tables (Acts 6:2). The close connection of the qualifications for deacons and the qualifications of pastor-elders in 1 Timothy 3 also suggests the same arrangement. The deacons were to assist the elders (who replaced the apostles as the spiritual leaders of the church) with the physical needs of the church.

The qualifications in 1 Timothy imply this supporting role for deacons in two ways. Deacons are not required to have the "ability to teach," although this does not preclude them from doing so. At least two of the seven in Acts, Stephen and Philip, were very active in preaching and evangelism (Acts 7–8). In addition, the qualifications are not quite as rigorous for deacons as they are for pastor-elders.

The role of the seven in Acts is clearly spelled out. They were to be in charge of the "daily serving of food" (NASB) to the widows. The church inherited this charitable practice from the Jews. The synagogue had a regular organization to help those in need. They preferred to give their alms for the poor through the synagogue rather than doing it individually. Barclay describes this practice:

Each Friday in every community two official collectors went round the markets and called on each house, collecting donations for the poor and needy in money and goods. This material so collected was distributed to those in need by a committee . . . The poor of the community were given enough food for fourteen meals, that is for two meals a day for the week. But no one could receive any donation from this fund if he already possessed a week's food in the house. This fund . . . was called the kuppah, or the basket. In addition, there was a daily collection of food from house to house for those who were actually in emergency need for the day. This fund was called the tamhui or the tray.[27]

It was this practice that the first deacons inherited and performed. At first the money for the poor had been administered or at least supervised by the apostles (Acts 4:35), but when the number of the disciples grew to five thousand men (Acts 4:4), the job became too much for them, and deacons were elected to help.

Another indication of the deacon's role is inherent in the name itself: "servant." Just as the title *bishop* carries with it the job description of "overseer" and the title *pastor* means a "shepherd," one who takes care of the flock, the title *deacon* refers to one who serves. This does not mean that it is a lowly or unimportant office. The qualifications are quite high. They indicate that the deacon must be morally pure, spiritually mature, doctrinally strong, and able to handle money responsibly. In addition, he must be a good example in his family life and his deportment in the community. He is one to be respected in the church.

No other directions are given in Scripture concerning the work of the deacon. One thing is clear: it is not the job of the deacon to rule the church. Just as there is no such thing in Scripture as a board of elders, there is no such thing as a board of deacons. Authority in the church comes from the Lord to the congregation. Deacons may be authorized by the congregation to serve the church in various ways, but these should be under the same headings found in Scripture. They should help the pastor or pastors with their ministry and help meet the physical needs of the congregation. Lea and Griffin conclude from 1 Timothy 3:8–13 that "deacons likely served in an undefined way to assist the overseer, but they may not have been deeply involved in church financial affairs."[28] The Constitution of the Presbyterian Church of the USA defines the role of the deacon more broadly. It says that the deacon: "shall minister to those in need, to the sick, to the friendless, and to any who may be in distress . . . To this board may be delegated . . . responsibilities relating to the oversight of members, to the finances and properties of the church, and to its evangelistic, missionary, and educational programs."[29]

Deacons may be involved properly in all of these ministries as appointed by the church, but Strauch is correct when he says that "deacons are the church's ministers of mercy."[30] Whatever else they do in serving God and His church, they should be careful not to neglect their primary ministry of service to the needy. No spiritual gifts are listed in the qualifications for deacons, but it seems reasonable that a deacon's gifts should be appropriate for his ministry. If that be the case, then the church should look for those who have the gift of "helping" (1 Cor. 12:28) or the gift of "showing mercy" (Rom. 12:8). Without these gifts deacons will not be as effective in fulfilling the ministry to which God has appointed them.

Number of Deacons

The New Testament does not give any directions concerning the number of deacons a church should have. Perhaps no fixed number is given because churches of different sizes with differing conditions have very different needs for the deacons' ministry. The Jerusalem church consisted of five thousand men and perhaps as many as twenty thousand believers (Acts 4:4) at the time they chose seven to be deacons. That was a ratio of almost three thousand people per deacon. Using these figures, one could conclude that most churches have too many deacons.

There is another practical consideration. When handling money, it should be required that at least two deacons are involved. This was required by the Jews of those who collected money for the poor. It does two things. (1) It removes the temptation to take money from the collection for personal matters. (2) It removes any cause for accusation against the deacon if there is ever a problem because there are witnesses to his faithfulness. It is good to do these things openly so there is no question about honesty or unfairness with the use of church funds.

Finally, a church should have no more deacons than there are men qualified to serve. One of the most serious problems a church can have is deacons or a pastor-elder who does not meet the qualifications set forth in Scripture. This is a form of disobedience to God in electing the unqualified or not taking seriously the dictates of Scripture in these matters. It results in at least two problems. (1) It is a bad example to the younger members. Disregarding Scripture in this way says to them that it is not really important to obey Scripture in other ways. (2) It results in weak spiritual leadership for the church. If the church has mediocre leaders, it will become a mediocre church. The requirements for a deacon are very demanding because God wants the church to be a "holy nation" (1 Pet. 2:9), ones who have "purified your souls in obeying the truth" (1 Pet. 1:22).

Conclusion

Deacons have a very important role in the church. Although they are "servants" and their ministry is a ministry of service, the fact that they have been chosen demonstrates they are respected by the brethren. Their role is second in importance only to the pastor-elders. The pastor(s) are given by the Lord the responsibility of teaching the Word. Without this ministry the church will not prosper spiritually. Part of the duty of the deacons is to relieve the pastor-elders of responsibilities that would keep them from doing their best in studying the Word, spending time alone with God in prayer, and teaching the Word effectively. This is the reason the first deacons were chosen (Acts 6). Deacons still need to work closely with the pastor-elder(s) to make sure that this problem does not arise. Many churches are hampered in their spiritual development because the pastor-elder has "laid down" the Word of God to do other things.

The deacon is not described as a "ruler" in the church. However, as one who assists the "overseers" of the church and is appointed by the church to fulfill specific ministries, the deacon is by virtue of his office a leader of the church. His value to the church is in his service. He is not to be the pastor-elder's supervisor but his helper. Deacons are not to form a board to rule the church; that is not their job description. They are to lead the church in ministry. Churches who have such deacons will be blessed indeed. Pastors who have such deacons to help them will be better pastors because of it. Deacons who serve well "obtain for themselves a good standing and great boldness in the faith" (1 Tim. 3:13).

Ecclesiology in the Free Churches of the Reformation (1525–1608)

Emir E. Caner
Assistant Professor of Church History
and Anabaptist Studies
Southeastern Baptist Theological Seminary

On a cold, winter evening in Zurich, Switzerland, a group of young men quietly plodded through the snow and assembled at the home of Felix Mantz. Disgruntled at the slow progress of the Reformation under the leadership of Ulrich Zwingli (A.D. 1484–1531), this group of radicals was about to take a step which would forever separate them from Zwingli and his state-run reform. Indeed, their boldness would sever ties with Magisterial Reformers including Martin Luther (A.D. 1483–1546) and John Calvin (A.D. 1509–1564), who placed the authority of sacred matters in the hands of princes and town councils.

That night a dozen or so men huddled inside a small home to discern the will of God in their lives. An eye-witness account explains the monumental act which occurred next:

> And it came to pass that they were together until anxiety came upon them, yes, they were so pressed within their hearts. Thereupon they began to bow

their knees to the Most High God in heaven and
called upon him as the Informer of Hearts, and
they prayed that he would give to them his divine
will and that he would show his mercy unto them.
For flesh and blood and human forwardness did
not drive them, since they well knew what they
would have to suffer on account of it.

After the prayer, George of the House of Jacob
stood up and besought Conrad Grebel for God's
sake to baptize him with the true Christian baptism
upon his faith and knowledge. And when he knelt
down with such a request and desire, Conrad baptized him, since at that time there was no ordained
minister to perform such work.[1]

Over the next three years, most of the men that gathered that providential night, given the derogatory name
Anabaptist ("rebaptizer"), were martyred for the faith.
Conrad Grebel (A.D. 1498–1526) died of the plague, a
direct result of rat fleas which bit him in prison. Felix
Mantz (A.D. 1500–1527) was executed by his former
mentor Ulrich Zwingli via drowning. George Blaurock
(A.D. 1492–1528) was burned at the stake eighteen months
later by Catholic authorities.

Yet what caused such strong reaction was not any sote-
riological heresy among the Anabaptists. Without question, Anabaptists held to the doctrine of justification by
faith alone. They affirmed fundamental doctrines such as
Sola Scriptura (Scripture alone as authoritative and sufficient), the Tri-unity of the Godhead, and the deity of Jesus
Christ. The reason for the bloodshed was essentially *ecclesiological*. Anabaptists would not recognize the right of
the state in church matters. While Zwingli allowed the
town council to decide issues of eternal significance, the

Anabaptists believed that only the people of God through the Spirit of God had that right.

Baptism was the most visible expression of this belief in the authority of the believer's church. This ordinance, as the New Testament demonstrates, is an act only to be given to those candidates who voluntarily and intelligibly profess their decision to follow Jesus Christ as Savior and Lord. Thereby, it could not be given to infants. However, when Anabaptists rejected infant baptism, they also rejected citizenship into the city-state, a crime punishable by death. They were considered anarchists by the Magisterial Reformers, though these personal pacifists supported the right of the state to uphold civil law and order. In reality, Magisterial Reformers and Roman Catholics martyred Anabaptists not because of (re)baptism, but because they freed the church from the grip of the state. Anabaptists boldly gave their lives not only as a witness for the Lord but also for His church—a church which they believed must be free from the fetters of the state in order to regain its purity and build itself upon the authority of the Word of God. They died over the doctrine of the church.

Today, the doctrine of the church has once more materialized as a topic of debate. Yet it is not the struggle of authority between state and church which is reemerging but the question of authority *within* the church. As the state has lost its power over most churches, Christians now struggle with who, under the headship of Christ, is given the biblical authority to rule on matters of faith. Thankfully, the Anabaptists, the Free Church of the Reformation, again become a wealth of information and insight from which to draw insight. Their thoroughly biblical model of authority and leadership is an example for

the pressing issues of our day. The following section, therefore, is dedicated to surveying the ecclesiological movement of sixteenth-century Anabaptism through its major
figures and confessions.

Restoring the New Testament Church: Early Anabaptism's Formation of the Church (1525)

Conrad Grebel, who during his formative years of
humanistic college education was known as a womanizer
and brawler, was converted to Christ under the ministry of
Zwingli. Indeed, for eighteen months after his conversion,
Grebel strongly supported the leadership of his mentor,
including Zwingli's refutation against the veneration of
images and the Catholic view of the mass. But the separation between teacher and pupil occurred over the doctrine
of a believer's church. Grebel believed that a fellowship
should be made up exclusively of regenerate members of
the body of Christ while Zwingli held to an inclusivistic
view of the church composed of believers (wheat) and
unbelievers (tares).[2]

Grebel and other Anabaptist leaders, ever aware of the
strident opposition of the town council in Zurich, moved
the Anabaptist movement to Zollikon, a small village just
south of Zurich. In fact, during the first months of the radical movement, it became the center of Anabaptist activity.
Here, Blaurock preached numerous times, while Grebel
was known to have held communion shortly after the
January baptismal service. Reacting against the episcopal
and presbyterian hierarchical structure of state-run
churches, the Anabaptists asserted that the New
Testament only affirmed one form of church government—congregational rule.

Though pastoral authority was essential to the survival of the movement, primitive Anabaptism nonetheless heralded and defended an autonomous form of church government. As one Mennonite scholar explained, "It was the principle of the Anabaptists to have their congregations function in a democratic way in contrast to the large state churches, which had a somewhat episcopal form of church government, operating usually from the top down."[3] This congregational order was further illustrated by the simplistic church structure made up of the two New Testament offices: elder/bishop, who was authorized by the local assembly to perform all church functions, and deacon (sometimes called "servants of the poor").[4]

Congregational Rule:
Balthasar Hubmaier,
Theologian of Anabaptism (1526)

In the spring of 1522, an experienced Roman Catholic priest by the name of Balthasar Hubmaier (1480–1528) was wrestling with his own faith and the authority on which it was based. Hubmaier, who was the only Anabaptist with an earned doctor of theology degree, was serving a parish in Waldshut, Germany. He began an intense study of the Scriptures and came to the same conclusion as Martin Luther: "The just shall live by faith." Rejecting the tradition and pomp of his church, Hubmaier initiated reform at his own parish similar to the change being brought about by Zwingli at the Grossmunster Church.

Over time Hubmaier's desire to follow scriptural principles exceeded Zwingli's cautious stance on reform. Since Roman Catholic tradition was an obstacle to the Magisterial Reformers, Zwinglian compromise was eventually a barrier to the Anabaptists. This is nowhere as apparent as it was in the doctrine of the church. On numerous occasions Hubmaier and Zwingli clashed over ecclesiological issues, especially regarding baptism and its impact upon the believer and his local assembly. While Zwingli retained infant baptism as a sign of the Abrahamic Covenant, Hubmaier maintained that baptism must be preceded by a profession of faith from the candidate to the entire church.

In fact, though it was the responsibility of the pastor to examine the baptismal candidate doctrinally, the ultimate decision on whether someone could be baptized and join the church rested in the authority of its members. Hubmaier states:

> The bishop presents him to the church, calling on all brothers and sisters to fall to their knees, to call upon God with fervent devotion, that he might graciously impart to this person the grace and the power of his Holy Spirit and complete in him what he has begun through his Holy Spirit and divine Word. . . .
>
> After the church has completed this prayer, the bishop lays his hands on the head of the new member and says: "I testify to you and give you authority that henceforth you shall be counted among the Christian community, as a member participating in the use of her keys, breaking of bread and praying with other Christian sisters and brothers."[5]

The reason for the strict scrutiny of who should be baptized thus becomes obvious. The person baptized is now an equal member in like standing with the other members. The body of Christ, not any individual member or group such as elders, is granted the "keys" of authority from Christ Himself (Matt. 16:19).

Nowhere was this authority better demonstrated than in the area of church discipline ("the ban"), which was to be enforced upon those members who had strayed from God and walked unrepentantly into the open arms of sin. In fact, the normative Anabaptist viewed the ban from the community of God as the absolute worst punishment bestowed upon a Christian. According to Hubmaier, this power to discipline and restore backslidden members was given to the congregation itself:

> Now sisters and brothers, before they gather for the Supper, must be registered and have authority over each other, for one must have admonished the sinner twice beforehand. Where does this authority come from, if not from the pledge of baptism?[6]

Expounding from 1 Corinthians 5, Hubmaier argued that the church, not the pope or an episcopal oligarchy, is justified biblically to authorize the exclusion of a Christian. In the end Hubmaier hoped that this disciplinary measure would allow the sinner to examine himself, desist from sin, and thereby be welcomed back into the very same fellowship that excluded him at one time.

A Strong Yet Balanced Pastoral Authority: Michael Sattler and the Schleitheim Confession of 1527

As Hubmaier was crystallizing his convictions in Moravia, Michael Sattler (1490–1527), a former Benedictine monk turned Anabaptist evangelist, was calling on Anabaptist leaders from across Europe to come together, settle issues of disagreement, and defend Anabaptist theology from its critics. In February 1527, these leaders gathered in Schleitheim, Switzerland, uniting the young movement under seven major articles.

After issuing statements on baptism, church discipline, the Lord's Supper, and separation from the world, the confession turned its attention to the issue of pastoral authority. Though it is plain to see that the congregation has ultimate authority, the confession did confer strong pastoral leadership in order to guard the flock from corruption:

> The office of such a person shall be to read and exhort and teach, warn, admonish, or ban in the congregation, and properly to preside among the sisters and brothers in prayer, and in the breaking of bread, and in all things to take care of the body of Christ, that it may be built up and developed, so that the name of God might be praised and honored through us, and the mouth of the mocker stopped.[7]

It must be noted that this authority to ban came directly from the congregation, and ultimately was brought before the congregation. Simply put, the pastor guarded the purity of the church while the entire congregation publicly admonished the unrepentant member before communion "so that we may all in one spirit and in one love break and eat from one bread and drink from one cup."[8] In fact, the pastor himself could be disciplined by the congregation if necessary. The confession explained, "But should a shepherd do something worthy of reprimand, nothing shall be done with him without the voice of two or three witnesses. If they sin they shall be publicly reprimanded, so that others might fear."[9]

Both congregational rule and strong pastoral authority were essential to the survival of the embryonic movement.

Without strong leadership from the shepherd, novice Christians were left unequipped and unguarded from the dangers of the world. On the other hand, countless Anabaptist churches lost their pastors by way of martyrdom. Therefore, if the pastor had carried ultimate authority, the church would have lost its power every time it lost its pastor. Instead, the Schleitheim Confession affirmed that "if the shepherd should be driven away or led to the Lord by the cross, at the same hour another shall be ordained to his place, so that the little folk and the little flock of God may not be destroyed, but be preserved by warning and be consoled."[10] Ultimately, this confession demonstrated an incredible balance between two parties who are dependent on each other. Ironically, only three months after this document was finished, Michael Sattler, its chief architect, was executed by the Catholic authorities for heresy and sedition.

The Call of the Church, the Call of Its Preacher: Menno Simons's Foundation of Christian Doctrine (1539–1540, revised 1554)

In 1535 a respected Catholic priest stood quietly by as three hundred Anabaptists were put to death near his cloister in Pingjum, the Netherlands. The scene proved gut-wrenching to his soul as he sympathized with men and women who were willing to give their lives for their faith. In fact, the executions en masse were all the more atrocious when he realized that his very own brother was one of those executed for the heresy of rebaptism. Yet the bloodshed that day proved not only to be the turning point in this priest's life but, indeed, a turning point in the history of the Free Church.

Menno Simons (1496–1561) had long struggled with his Catholic faith and its biblical authority. When searching for the truth on topics such as baptism, he did not find respite in the modified doctrines of Magisterial Reformers who upheld much of Catholic ecclesiology. Instead it was the radical faith of the Anabaptists that opened his eyes to the truth of the gospel of grace. Simons, immediately following his conversion, committed his life to preaching the gospel of Christ. In fact, as he looked back upon his life lived in darkness, he recognized that his conversion to the Living Word was directly related to the preaching of the written Word:

> But Thou didst send Thy beloved Son, the dearest pledge of Thy grace, who preached Thy Word, fulfilled Thy righteousness, accomplished Thy will, bore our sins, blotted them out with Thy Blood, stilled Thy wrath, conquered the devil, hell, sin, and death, and obtained grace, mercy, favor, and peace for all who truly believe in Him. . . . He sent out His messengers preaching this peace . . . so that they might lead me and all erring sinners into the right way. . . . Their words I love, their practices I follow, Thy dear son, Christ Jesus, whom they preached to me, I believe. His will and way I seek.[11]

From that day forward Simons pledged to preach the Word of God, a calling he considered to be from God Himself.

Only three years later Simons published the first edition of his magnum opus entitled *Foundation of Christian Doctrine*. Therein Simons spends much time discussing the importance of the call on a preacher's life. Simons reminds his readers that the authority a preacher has does not come from man-made decisions or passions but by the divine summons given by God on his life, as was the case with Moses, Zechariah, Jeremiah, and Paul. Indeed, the authority a preacher has is directly correlated with the One who calls him. Simons explained:

> You see, my good reader, all they who by such a power are touched in their hearts, are driven by the Holy Ghost, are constrained by love to God and their neighbor, and all called by the Lord Himself, or by a church without fault, believing and Christian, rightly to teach in the house of God, that is, to teach in the church of Jesus Christ, with sound doctrine and by a pious and unblamable conduct, to admonish, rebuke or reprove, and comfort, and assist in paternal love, to administer the Lord's holy baptism and Supper rightly, to ward off diligently with God's Word all seducing and false teachers, and to exclude all incurable members from the communion of the godly, etc. To such Christ says, As my Father hath sent me, even so send I you. Without such a vocation no one can ever rightly preach the Gospel, as Paul says, How shall they preach except they be sent.[12]

It is clear that the pastor's authority primarily rested within his calling from God. Furthermore, it must be noted that the church also played an integral role in the authority of the pastor, as they had the final decision on whether to call him and bestow him with authority in regards to their congregation.

Simons believed that those who were not sent by God were profiteering from the people of God. He wrote, "Their service is vain, their labor without fruit, yes, it is nothing but sowing by the seashore and reaping the wind."[13] Simons reminded his readers that no one should selfishly desire the office of pastor without the calling on his life. Those who wished to be pastors in their own power, he explained, would have a dreadful end: "Ah, dear sirs, awake and fear God, for the hour draws near that your moments of laughter will be changed into an endless lament, this fleeting joy into eternal sorrow, and this moment of ease and luxury into death and endless woe."[14]

As opposed to a false preacher residing within a false church, Simons's view of a true church began with a fellowship of saved individuals. He maintained:

[The church of Christ], from the beginning have
firmly trusted and believed in the promised Seed of
the woman, which is the promised Prophet,
Messiah, Shiloh, King, Prince, Emmanuel, and
Christ; who accepted His word in sincerity of
heart, follow His example, are led by His Spirit,
and who trust in His promise in the Scripture.[15]

Such a high view of the assembly explicitly led then to a congregational rule of the body.[16] Simons emphasized that God's people, the bride of Christ with a Spiritual King, have privileges given to them which include:

1. *Priesthood of the Believer.* "Their sword is the sword of the Spirit, which they wield in a good conscience through the Holy Ghost."

2. *Believer's Baptism.* "Their baptism they administer to the believing according to the commandment of the Lord."

3. *Memorial Lord's Supper.* "Their Lord's Supper they celebrate as a memorial of the favors and death of their Lord, and an incitement to brotherly love."

4. *Church Discipline.* "Their ban or excommunication descends on all the proud scorners—great and small, rich and poor, without any respect to persons."[17]

The key to Simons's ecclesiology is that believers in Christ have been made pure and, thereby, are endowed with the power over the keys to the kingdom. Simons is clear that the authority of the church is found within its people, its congregation. Through God's "unadulterated Word," His ordinances, His preachers, and His bishops, the people of God are sufficiently warned of the wiles of the devil and can make biblical decisions which will please the One whom they serve.

Bridging Continental Anabaptism with English Baptists: The Waterlander Confession of 1580

Upon Menno's death in 1561, Dutch Anabaptists came to a crucial crossroads in their future. The successor to Simons, Dirk Philips, exercised church discipline upon respected leaders among the Mennonites, using little caution along the way. As a result, the Mennonites split into three major groups, each emerging according to the view of church discipline enforced. The more sympathetic Anabaptists, known as the Waterlanders due to their location in northern Holland, rejected the heavy-handed tactics of Philips. Instead they sought a balanced view of discipline as well as other areas of ecclesiology and drew up a confession of faith in 1580.

Through the able leadership of their pastor, Hans de Ries (1553–1638), the Waterlander Church in Middleburg set forth forty articles of faith. Thirty years later the confession was reprinted at the request of John Smyth, an English Separatist whose group would make up the first

General Baptist Church in the world. In fact, when Smyth died in 1612, the majority of his congregation joined the Waterlander Church.

Within the Waterlander Church there were two main offices: bishop and deacon. Since bishops were called to pastor several churches at one time, the confession also mentioned the ministry of the teacher, whose sole function was to preach the Word "mostly in his own congregation, while the elders were traveling extensively in the various congregations of their respective districts."[18] Indeed, the vast majority of these men were truly pastors in training, eventually given the opportunity to shepherd a flock. Hence, any distinction between elder and teacher soon disappeared within the ranks of the Waterlander Church.

The perpetuity of the local church was essential in the doctrine of the Waterlanders. Therefore, the election of a pastor or deacon, for which the congregation took responsibility, carried great significance. Article 27 explained:

> Calling or election to the aforesaid ministries is accomplished through the ministers of the church and its members conjointly (a), and by invocation of the name of God; for God alone knows hearts, walks in the midst of the believers (b), who are congregated in his name, and through his Holy Spirit directs their intellects and minds so that through them he manifests and calls forth such as he knows will be useful to his church.[19]

As is stated repeatedly, God endows the congregation with spiritual minds in order to discern His will in their midst. Moreover, they can be assured that those who are organized under the banner of Christ will have His wisdom bestowed upon them through the Holy Spirit. Ultimately, congregationalism is the conduit in which God works best.

It is this system which triumphs as the people of God come together and seek His counsel.

After the election the pastor is ordained to the ministry by the laying on of hands from other pastors. He is commanded to carry out the task "which Jesus Christ brought from heaven."[20] Furthermore, his life should model the life of Christ that is found within the sacred Scriptures. With such a high standard, the pastor can find solace in his calling from God and the affirmation of his calling and ability by the church.

A Godly Pulpit Through a Godly Pew: The Ecclesiological Legacy of the Anabaptists

The delicate and biblical balance between the shepherd and the flock is most evident within the life of the sixteenth-century Anabaptist church. Believing that they had been called by God to restore the New Testament church, Anabaptists guarded the fellowship from false teachers and false doctrine. They ensured the purity of the church through believer's baptism, the Lord's Supper, and church discipline.

The one most responsible for carrying out this task was the pastor himself. It was his duty to diligently search the Scriptures each week and share with his flock the bread of life. He was called to cast the vision of the church in the way God led him. Therefore, the congregation took special care to find a bishop whose life emulated the life of Christ and whose heart illustrated the love of Christ. This was a corporate responsibility, not a selective one. God had called them out of the world together. They were to serve together. They were the church of God whose responsibility was to spread the gospel to the corners of the earth.

Consequently, their leader must be one who not only could be followed but should be honored as well. Indeed, he is a servant among servants who is given authority from God and the congregation. If he were ever to stumble morally or theologically, he himself would face the same discipline by the congregation that he recommended for others. But if he worked vigorously to give the people of God the Word of God, if he lived in such a way that others could follow him, he was given the admiration due him.

Ultimately, the decisive example of the congregation and pastor working together came through martyrdom. Suffering together created an eternal bond considered by Anabaptists as the "third baptism." As one Anabaptist hymn stated:

> Therefore, let us praise God
> Who gives humankind such grace
> and power from on high,
> Who wants to make us worthy of victory,
> along with all the saints,
> So that we win the crown when we are
> put to the test,
> As we have witnessed that they have done.[21]

Ecclesiology Among Baptists in Great Britain and America (1609–Present)

Stephen Prescott

Faculty in Church History

Southeastern College at Wake Forest

British and English Baptists have never regarded ecclesiology as the most important of all doctrines. Without doubt, theology proper, Christology, soteriology, and probably Bibliology—or the doctrine of the authority and reliability of the Scripture—would all be counted more important in Baptist history and theology. However, ecclesiology is what separates Baptists from other orthodox Christian groups—what makes them Baptists—and that for which they are best known. Indeed, the very name *Baptist* comes from one aspect of their ecclesiology, a believer's church composed of a membership of born-again individuals who have submitted to the ordinance of baptism by immersion as a symbol of both the death, burial, and resurrection of Christ, and of the believer's death to sin and self, and his resurrection to new life in Christ. Baptists' distinctive ecclesiological convictions have been a hallmark of Baptist life and theology in both Britain and the United States.

Like Catholics and Protestants, Baptists ascribe to Nicene and Chalcedonian orthodoxy and would rate the Trinity and the deity of Christ as the foremost doctrines. Like the Magisterial Reformers of the Reformation Era, Baptists accept salvation by grace through faith and the authority and sufficiency of the Scripture in all matters of faith and practice. Baptists share with Protestants the distinctive doctrines of *sola Scriptura, sola fide,* and *sola sacerdos.* However, what is unique about Baptists, what separates them from the Magisterial Reformers, is their doctrine of church: regenerate membership, believer's baptism, congregational rule, one office of teaching (the elder/pastor/bishop, called of God to that ministry and elected by the people of a congregation as their minister), a lay office of helps known as deacons, and decisions on good standing and discipline of both members and ministers made by the church as a whole.

Lacking a hierarchy or an authoritative curia, there is no "official" body or leader to state Baptist beliefs. Baptists have neither a pope nor church councils to expound authoritative dogma, believing the Bible to be the only source of authority. Of course, all Christian groups profess to follow the Bible. There is a need to delineate what Baptists believe for three purposes: to instruct new members, to inform those outside the Baptist faith, and to provide a basis of fellowship. Historically Baptist churches have published their doctrinal beliefs in confessions of faith, initially by individual congregations, and soon after by local associations or other Baptist organizations. Thus, I have analyzed various Baptist confessions to trace Baptist ecclesiology over the centuries, using William L. Lumpkin's *Baptist Confessions of Faith* as the source of these confessions.[1]

Early General Baptists
and Their Confessions of Faith

The origin of the first recorded English-speaking Baptist church is well-known.[2] In 1606, the Separatist congregation in Gainsborough, England, divided into separate congregations for reasons of safety due to persecution of religious dissenters by the first Stuart king, James I. In 1607 one of the Gainsborough congregations, under the leadership of the minister John Smyth and the prominent and wealthy layman Thomas Helwys, immigrated to Holland to escape the Stuart persecution. The adult men in the church began to work for an Anabaptist merchant, Jan Munter, baking hardtack at Munter's East India Bakehouse. Almost immediately Smyth began conversations both with Anabaptists and another English Separatist congregation known as the Ancient Church that had also fled to Holland to avoid persecution. The Ancient Church had rejected Presbyterian polity and instituted congregational rule. They refused, however, to accept believer's baptism, a point that Smyth debated with them. In 1609, convinced that salvation followed by believer's baptism should be the basis of church membership, John Smyth baptized first himself and then the other members of the church. Thus, the first English-speaking Baptist church was born in Holland. Arminian and Anabaptist in soteriology, these Baptists are known as General Baptists based on their belief in the general or unlimited atonement.

John Smyth and the
Short Confession of Faith
in Twenty Articles (1609)

John Smyth wrote the first English Baptist confession of faith in 1609. It is distinctively Baptist, not Separatist in its ecclesiology. Lumpkin notes of Smyth's confession: "Indeed, the confession is unique among English Separatist confessions prior to 1610 in two respects: it was anti-Calvinistic and anti-pedobaptist."[3] Although it was the first Baptist confession in English, it reflects a full-orbed Baptist ecclesiology. Article 12 limits the church to regenerate persons who have been baptized "after the confession of sin and faith."[4] Article 13 provides for congregational rule, including in the matter the appointment and dismissal of ministers. It states that the last appeal is always to the body of the church.

Smyth's confession specified two offices within the church, one of ministering the word and ordinances, the other of serving and attending to the needs of the poor or sick. Interestingly, he used neither the term *elder*, the most common term in the New Testament and Baptist practice, nor the synonymous term *pastor* that has been popular for the last half-century, but rather *bishop (episkopos)* for the teaching office of the church.

> That the ministers of the church are, not only bishops ("Episcopos"), to whom the power is given of dispensing both the word and the sacraments, but also deacons, men and widows, who attend to the affairs of the poor and sick brethren.[5]

Thomas Helwys and the Declaration of Faith of English People Remaining at Amsterdam in Holland (1611)

John Smyth and Thomas Helwys soon parted company over Smyth's decision to seek membership in a Waterlander church. Most of the church followed Helwys's leadership, and in 1611 the church decided to return to England to bear witness to its own people and nation. Shortly before leaving for England, Helwys wrote a confession of faith for the English Baptists entitled "A Declaration of Faith of English People Remaining at Amsterdam in Holland."[6] Already, the ecclesiology and polity of this first English-speaking Baptist congregation was the traditional Baptist ecclesiology of Smyth's confession.

The membership of the church is composed of regenerate, baptized persons only (article 10). There are two offices in the church, elder and deacon (article 20). Elders "feed the flock concerning their souls," deacons "relieve the necessities of the poor and impotent brethren concerning their bodies."[7] These officers are chosen by "election and approbation of that church or congregation whereof they are members." These Baptists explicitly rejected Calvin's tripartite division of teaching elders, ruling elders, and deacons: "And there being but one rule for Elders, therefore but one sort of Elders."[8]

Early Particular Baptists and Their Confessions of Faith

As noted earlier, the first English Baptists had been Arminians, people who believed that Christ had died for the sins of all the world, that God desired all men to be saved, that He offered salvation to all, and that all could be saved. These Baptists took the name General Baptists. During the 1630s there arose in England Particular Baptists, persons of Calvinistic soteriology who believed that God had chosen only some for eternal life and only those could be saved. While the Particular Baptists rejected the Anabaptist soteriology of the General Baptists in favor of a Reformed soteriology, they did not accept a Reformed ecclesiology.

In 1644 seven of the Particular Baptist congregations within London decided to prepare a joint confession of faith, both to answer accusations of Pelagianism and anarchy leveled against them and to distinguish themselves from Anabaptists and General Baptists. This first Particular Baptist Confession, known as the First London Confession, was based on a 1596 confession probably prepared by Henry Ainsworth.[9] Some have contended that the First London Confession is the most important confession of faith in Baptist history. I would assign that distinction to the New Hampshire Confession of Faith of 1833. Whichever is given the primacy, the First London Confession is doubtless highly influential in Baptist life. A second edition was issued in 1646, a third edition in 1651, a fourth edition in 1652, and a fifth edition in 1653. These later editions moderate even further the already moderate Calvinism of the confession,[10] affirm the principle of freedom of religion, and clarify the offices of the church.

Church membership is limited to regenerate persons who have undergone believer's baptism (article 23).[11] The first edition of the Confession stated in article 36 that "every church has the power given them from Christ for their better well-being, to choose to themselves meet persons into the office of Pastors, teachers, elders, Deacons."[12] Pastors, teachers, and elders could be read as one or three offices. Any ambiguity was corrected; the second, third, fourth, and fifth editions all dropped the words *pastors* and *teachers,* giving the church the right to choose for its offices elders and deacons. Discipline of errant members was likewise a matter of discernment for the whole church (article 43).[13]

General Baptists and the
Standard Confession (1660)

In 1660 the Puritan government ended ignominiously, and Charles II was soon to be recalled from France to resume the Stuart rule that had been terminated twenty-one years earlier with the execution of his father. The English General Baptists met in London in March of that year. Although disproportionately composed of persons from the London area, this group had a national composition. They prepared a doctrinal statement for the English General Baptists that was presented to Charles II on July 26, 1660. The document itself was entitled "A Brief Confession or Declaration of Faith," but it is universally known today as the Standard Confession of 1660. The Standard Confession is for English General Baptists what the First London Confession is for English Particular Baptists—their foremost statement of faith.

The Standard Confession recognizes two offices within the local church:

> That the Elders or Pastors which God hath
> appointed to oversee, and feed his Church (consti-
> tuted as aforesaid) are such, who first being of the
> number of Disciples, shall in time appear to *be vig-
> ilant, sober, of good behavior, given to hospitality,
> apt to teach, etc. not greedy of filthy lucre* (as too
> many National Ministers are) *but patient; not a
> brawler, not covetous, etc.* and as such chose, and
> ordained to office (according to the order of
> Scripture, *Acts 14:23* who are to feed the flock
> with meat in due season, and in much love to rule
> over them, with all care).[14]

This passage indicates that God calls men to the ministry, but the church chooses the God-called man whom they believe God would have minister to them. Deacons, chosen by the church and ordained by prayer, and "laying on of hands" direct and coordinate all the members in relieving the distress of the poor (article 19). Discipline is by the church (article 17).[15]

American Baptist Confessions of Faith

Like their English cousins, Baptists in America have written a multiplicity of confessions to delineate what they believe.[16] However, two are by far the most important: The Philadelphia Confession of Faith of 1742 and the New Hampshire Confession of Faith of 1833. In the twentieth century the Southern Baptist Convention has become the largest Baptist body in the country (and the world). Its confession, the Baptist Faith and Message, was first adopted in 1925 and then slightly revised in 1963, 1998, and 2000. The Baptist Faith and Message is now the most widely known and most widely adopted of all Baptist confessions. However, it is based on the New Hampshire Confession. All three of these pivotal confessions of Baptists in America share the distinctive ecclesiological doctrines of the English Baptists.

Philadelphia Confession of Faith (1742)

Elias Keach, a Particular Baptist minister in both America and England, first published a confession of faith in 1697. Known as Keach's Confession, it circulated widely on both sides of the Atlantic. Keach made minor changes in at least five editions that were published sporadically. Keach's Confession, with some small changes, was adopted by the Philadelphia Baptist Association on September 25, 1742, and published as the Confession of the Association.[17] Chapter 27, paragraphs 8 and 9 specify the offices of the church.

8. A particular church gathered, and completely organized, according to the mind of Christ, consists of officers and members: and the officers appointed by Christ to be chosen and set apart by the Church (so called and gathered) for the peculiar administration of ordinances and execution of power or duty, which He entrusts them with or calls them to, to be continued to the end of the world, are bishops or elders, and deacons.

9. The way appointed by Christ for the calling of any person, fitted and gifted by the Holy Spirit, unto the office of bishop or elder in the Church, is that he be chosen thereunto by the common suffrage of the Church itself; and solemnly set apart by fasting and prayer, with imposition of hands of the eldership of the Church, if there be any before constituted therein; and of a deacon, that he be chosen by the like suffrage, and set apart by prayer, and the imposition of hands.[18]

The Philadelphia Confession also taught a regenerate church membership and congregational church discipline.

New Hampshire Confession of Faith (1833)

Apparently desiring a less Calvinistic statement of faith, the Baptist Convention of New Hampshire appointed a committee on June 24, 1830, to draft a new confession. The New Hampshire Confession of Faith was adopted and published in 1833. For twenty years it was not well-known outside New England. However, in 1853, J. Newton Brown revised it and published it in his book, *The Baptist Church Manual*. It soon became the most widely known and most widely used confession among American Baptists. In 1867, J. M. Pendleton included it in

his *Church Manual*. It thus became very influential among
Landmark Baptists. In 1925, with ten additional sections
and minor alterations, it was adopted by the Southern
Baptist Convention as the Baptist Faith and Message of
1925. In 1933 the General Association of Baptist
Churches adopted it. Most independent Baptist groups
such as the Baptist Bible Fellowship use the New
Hampshire Confession or a confession closely based on it.
It is unquestionably the most important American Baptist
confession and arguably the most important Baptist confession of all.

The New Hampshire Confession shares the ecclesiology
of the earlier Baptist confessions. The church is composed
of regenerate persons who have submitted to believer's
baptism. The church is governed by congregational rule,
and in it there are two offices. Interestingly, the New
Hampshire Confession states of a Gospel Church in article
11 that "its only proper offices are bishops or pastors, and
deacons."[19] The 1925 Baptist Faith and Message altered
the terminology slightly. In article 12, A Gospel Church
states, "Its Scriptural officers are bishops or elders and
deacons."[20] The 1963 (and 2000) edition changes the
nomenclature slightly: "Its Scriptural offices are pastors
and deacons."[21] Baptists, following what they believe to be
the teaching of the New Testament, have historically used
the terms *bishop, elder,* and *pastor* interchangeably and
treat this as one office.

The Current Ecclesiological Confusion

From the very beginning of English-speaking Baptist
life, ecclesiology has been a distinctive and largely non-
controversial doctrine. The church is composed of a regenerate membership that has followed the Lord in believer's

baptism. Church government is congregational. There are two offices: pastor or elder, and deacon. Pastors are called of God to the ministry and elected by the people. Deacons are laymen who attend to the physical needs of the congregation. Church membership and church discipline are matters for the church as a whole. Over the last thirty or forty years, some Baptist churches have moved from Baptist ecclesiology to a Presbyterian or Reformed doctrine.

One of these areas of doctrinal change is in church membership. In the 1960s, a number of Baptist churches in the state of North Carolina began to accept members who had been sprinkled as children. These persons, presumably, professed conversion but had not been baptized as believers. In 1971 the Baptist State Convention of North Carolina refused to require believer's baptism as the basis of membership in a church in fellowship with the convention.[22] A few churches in other states accept pedobaptists as members.

Another, and probably more common, deviation from Baptist ecclesiology has also emerged, at least in some areas. Some Baptist churches have adopted Presbyterian polity. Three offices are recognized: the pastor or teaching elder, the ruling elder (usually without the contentious word *ruling*), and the deacon. The elders rule the church, making decisions on membership, staff, finances, and most other areas, sometimes with an opportunity for the church to "affirm" the decision without any discussion or debate.

There is likely a multiplicity of reasons for the shift from Baptist to Presbyterian ecclesiology among a minority of Baptist churches. The ecumenical movement may have contributed. The growth of Reformed theology among a portion of Baptist churches may have contributed.

Ecclesiology has not been a major issue and has received relatively little attention by Baptist theologians in the last three-quarters of a century.

Historically, Baptists may have disagreed on the fine points, but there has been general agreement on the basics of ecclesiology and church polity. The local church is composed of those who profess to have saving faith and who have been baptized, almost always by immersion after their salvation. The church has two officers, the pastor or elder, and deacons. The church is ruled democratically by the congregation, so all decisions on membership, the calling of pastors, and the admission and dismissal of members rest ultimately with the membership. Our Baptist forebears would not have declared these the most important doctrines. They did not think that disagreeing with them made one heterodox or carnal. It did, however, make one not a Baptist.

Endnotes

Introduction

1. George Barna, "Lay Teams Help Fill Leadership Voids," in *The Alabama Baptist,* 24 June 2002, 7.

2. See John MacArthur Jr., *Answering the Key Questions About Elders* (Panorama City, Calif.: Grace to You, 1984), and Alexander Strauch, *Biblical Eldership,* Rev. ed. (Littleton, Colo.: Lewis & Roth Publishers, 1995).

3. Barna, 7.

4. George Eldon Ladd, *A Theology of the New Testament,* rev. ed. (Grand Rapids: Wm. B. Eerdmans Publishing Company, 1993), 579.

5. Robert L. Saucy, *The Church in God's Program* (Chicago: Moody Press, 1972), 98.

Chapter 1, Defining a Pastor-Elder

1. Joseph Henry Thayer, *A Greek, English Lexicon of the New Testament,* 4th ed. (Edinburgh: T. & T. Clark, 1901), 535.

2. Dale A. Robbins, "What's the Difference Between Elders, Bishops, and Pastors," *http://www.victorious.org/chur42.htm:* accessed 7 June 2001.

3. J. B. Lightfoot, *St. Paul's Epistle to the Philippians* (London: Macmillan & Co., 1913), 95.

4. The word *aner* is on a few occasions used as inclusive of male and female persons, that is, mankind. In the vast majority of cases it refers to the male as separate from female. If the word is taken in its normal usage, it would mean that there were 5,000 men who were believers, not to mention their families.

5. James Moffatt, *The Revelation of St. John the Divine,* in the *Expositor's Greek Testament,* 5 vols. (Grand Rapids: Wm. B. Eerdmans Publishing Company, 1974 reprint), 348. See also William Barclay, *The Revelation of John,* vol. 1, *The Daily Bible Study* (Edinburgh: St. Andrew Press, 1959), 66–68.

Chapter 2, The Call of a Pastor-Elder

1. Melissa Wigington, "FTE Looks to Congregations to Recruit Young Clergy," in *Horizons* 4:2 (2001): 1.

2. David J. Wood, "Where Are the Younger Clergy?" in *The Christian Century,* 11 April 2001, 18.

3. Gary Friesen, with J. Robin Maxson, *Decision Making and the Will of God* (Portland: Multnomah Press, 1980), 313.

4. Ibid.

5. Ibid., 314.

6. Os Guinness, *The Call* (Nashville: Word Publishing, 1998), 33.

7. Ibid., 43.

8. Ibid., 50.

9. James M. George, "The Call to Pastoral Ministry," in *Rediscovering Pastoral Ministry,* ed. John MacArthur Jr. (Dallas: Word, 1995), 102.

10. Ibid., 108.

11. W. A. Criswell, *Criswell's Guidebook for Pastors* (Nashville: Broadman Press, 1980), 345.

12. Erwin Lutzer, "Still Called to the Ministry," in *Moody Monthly,* March 1983, 133.

13. Ibid.

14. C. H. Spurgeon, *Lectures to My Students* (Grand Rapids: Zondervan, 1972 reprint), 22.

15. Thomas C. Oden, *Pastoral Theology* (San Francisco: Harper, 1983), 18.

16. John Calvin, *Institutes of the Christian Religion,* trans. John Allen (Grand Rapids: Wm. B. Erdmans Publishing Company, 1949 reprint), 2:326.

17. Francis Wayland, *Notes on the Principles and Practices of Baptist Churches* (New York: Sheldon and Co., 1859), 107.

Chapter 3, The Role of the Pastor-Elder

1. Saucy, 98ff.

2. Marvin E. Mayer, "An Exegetical Study on the New Testament Elder," Ph.D. diss., at Dallas Theological Seminary, 1970, 2.

3. William Barclay, *The Letters to Timothy, Titus, and Philemon* (Edinburgh: Saint Andrew Press, 1960), 84.

4. Mayer, 2.

5. George, 109–10.

6. Lightfoot, 194.

7. William F. Arndt and F. Wilbur Gingrich, *A Greek-English Lexicon of the New Testament and Other Early Christian Literature* (Chicago: University of Chicago Press, 1952), 306–307.

8. Ibid., 444.

9. See Gerhard Kittel, *Theological Dictionary of the New Testament,* trans. Geoffrey W. Bromiley (Grand Rapids: Wm. B. Eerdmans Publishing Company, 1944), 2:474, for the meaning of *elegcho.*

10. See Mayer, 164–65.

11. Arndt and Gingrich, 721.

12. Mayer, 114.

13. Alfred Plummer, *"The Pastoral Epistles,"* in *The Expositor's Bible,* ed. W. Robertson Nicoll (New York: Holder & Staughton, 1905), 32.

14. William Hendrickson, *Thessalonians, Timothy, and Titus,* in A New Testament Commentary (Grand Rapids: Baker Book House, 1979), 219.

15. F. F. Bruce, *The Book of the Acts,* in the New International Commentary (Grand Rapids: Wm. B. Eerdmans Publishing Co., 1977), 130. See also H. A. W. Meyer, *Acts,* trans. William Dickson, 2d ed., Commentary on the New Testament (Edinburgh: T. & T. Clark, 1889), 124–25.

16. See Arndt and Gingrich, 115.

17. John B. Polhill, *Acts,* in the New American Commentary (Nashville: Broadman Press, 1992), 430.

18. Arndt and Gingrich, 403.

19. Mayer, 142.

20. R. C. H. Lenski, *Hebrews and James* (Columbus, Ohio: Wartburg Press, 1934), 661–62. See also A. T. Robertson, *Word Pictures in the New Testament* (Nashville: Broadman Press, 1953), 6:64.

21. R. V. G. Tasker, *Epistle of James* (London: Tyndale Press, 1957), 129f.

22. The use of the subjunctive shows that it is possible that his sickness is a result of sin, but it does not say that *all* sickness is because of sin.

23. Timothy was not an evangelist, but he was told to "do the work of an evangelist" (2 Tim. 4:5). The Great Commission (Matt. 28:19–20) is for all believers.

24. Harvey E. Dana, *Manual of Ecclesiology* (Kansas City: Central Seminary Press, 1994), 254–55. Dana argues all other functions of the elder derive from this one. He says, "The chief function of this official was administrative. . . . He might sometimes 'labor in the Word and in teaching.'"

25. See the discussion on this subject in chapter 1. The passages where this term is used are 1 Peter 5:2 (verb form); 2:25; 1 Timothy 3:2; Acts 20:28; Titus 1:7; and Philippians 1:1.

26. Fenton John Anthony Hort, *The Christian Ecclesia* (London: Macmillan, 1914), 212.

27. James Hope Moulton and George Milligan, *The Vocabulary of the Greek Testament* (Grand Rapids: Wm. B. Eerdmans Publishing Company, 1982 reprint), 244.

28. Kittel, 2:615.

29. Arndt and Gingrich, 299.

30. Moulton and Milligan, 541.

31. Ibid.

32. Arndt and Gingrich, 713–14.

33. Robertson, 4:36.

34. Ibid., 4:404.

Chapter 4, The Qualifications for Pastor-Elders

1. George, 114.

2. Ibid.

3. Henry Martyn, *Journal and Letters of the Rev. Henry Martyn,* ed. S. Wilberforce (New York: M. W. Dodd, 1851).

4. Mayer, 55.

5. Hendrickson, 119.

6. Homer A. Kent, *The Pastoral Epistles* (Chicago: Moody Press, 1958), 121–30.

7. H. Harvey, *Commentary on the Pastoral Epistles,* in An American Commentary on the New Testament, ed. Alvah Hovey (Philadelphia: American Baptist Publication Society, 1890), 37.

8. Kent, 122.

9. See Craig S. Keener, . . . *And Marries Another* (Peabody, Mass.: Hendrickson Publishers, 1991), 87ff. for evidence on the practice of polygamy in the first century.

10. J. N. D. Kelly, *The Pastoral Epistles,* in Black's New Testament Commentaries (Peabody, Mass.: Hendrickson Publishers, 1960), 75.

11. Kent, 124.

12. Ibid., 123.

13. Plummer, 123.

14. Keener, 92–95.

15. Plummer, 125.

16. Kent, 123.

17. Keener, 94.

18. Ibid., 95.

19. Ibid.

20. Thomas D. Lea and Hayne Griffin Jr., *1, 2 Timothy and Titus*, New American Commentary (Nashville: Broadman Press, 1992), 109–10.

21. Kelly, 75.

22. Kent, 125.

23. Arland J. Hultgren, *I-II Timothy, Titus*, in the Augsburg Commentary on the New Testament (Minneapolis: Augsburg Publishing House, 1984), 73.

24. Warren W. Wiersbe, *The Bible Exposition Commentary* (Wheaton: Victor Books, 1989), 2:220.

25. Thayer, 425.

26. Moulton and Milligan, 426.

27. Henry George Liddell and Robert Scott, *A Greek-English Lexicon* (Oxford: Clarendon Press, 1996), 1,175.

28. Josephus, *Antiquities of the Jews* 3.12.2.

29. Barclay, 92.

30. Arndt and Gingrich, 810.

31. Barclay, 92.

32. Ibid., 93.

33. Ibid., 92.

34. Barclay, 93. See also Mayer, 61.

35. Moulton and Milligan, 356.

36. Kent, 127.

37. Mayer, 62.

38. Hendrickson, 124, and Patrick Fairbairn, *Commentary on the Pastoral Epistles* (Grand Rapids: Zondervan, 1956 reprint), 137–38, support this conclusion.

39. Thayer, 490.

40. Kent, 128.

41. Barclay, 91.

42. Arndt and Gingrich, 675.

43. Thayer, 516.

44. The next phrase, "not greedy for money," is not included in most Greek texts. It is very similar to the last qualification listed in this verse.

45. Thayer, 292.

46. Kelly, 77.

47. For a lengthy discussion on this concept, see Richard C. Trench, *Synonyms of the New Testament* (Grand Rapids: Wm. B. Eerdmans Publishing Company, 1953 reprint), 153–57.

48. Hendrickson, 126.

49. Mayer, 66.

50. Hendrickson, 127.

51. Ibid.

52. Trench, 381.

53. Barclay, 268.

54. Mayer, 75.

55. Barclay, 268.
56. Kent, 214.
57. Barclay, 270.
58. Ibid., 271.
59. Arndt and Gingrich, 24.
60. Kelly, 232.
61. Kent, 214.
62. Mayer, 79.
63. Arndt and Gingrich, 589.
64. Ibid., 215. See also Thayer, 167.
65. Kent, 215.
66. Mayer, 82.

Chapter 5, The Authority of the Pastor-Elder

1. Plummer, 108–17.
2. Ibid., 111.
3. Ibid., 107.
4. Saucy, 110.
5. Charles Ryrie, *Basic Theology* (Colorado Springs: Victor, 1996), 407.
6. Mark R. Brown, "Why I Came to a Three-Office View," http://search.msn.com/results.aspx?srch=105&FORM=AS5&q=Why+I+Came+to+the+Three-Office+View, accessed 23 May 2003.
7. E. R. Craven, ed., *The Constitution of the Presbyterian Church in the U.S.A.* (Philadelphia: Presbyterian Board of Publication, 1906), 354–55.
8. Ibid., 355–56.
9. Cleland Boyd McAfee, *The Ruling Elder* (Philadelphia: Presbyterian Board of Christian Education, 1931), 1. See also Eugene Carson Blake, ed., *Presbyterian Law for the Local Church,* rev. ed. (Philadelphia: Presbyterian Board of Christian Education, 1957).
10. Charles Hodge, *Discussions in Church Polity* (New York: Charles Scribner's Sons, 1878), 127–28.
11. A. T. Robertson, *Word Pictures in the New Testament* (Nashville: Broadman Press, 1931), 4:588.
12. Ibid., 36.
13. Hodge, 128.
14. Ibid.
15. Meyer, 188, 193–94.
16. Ibid., 102; see also 91.
17. Ibid., 187–88.
18. John F. Walvoord, *The Holy Spirit* (Findlay, Ohio: Dunham Publishing Company, 1958), 168.
19. The verb *kathizete* should be translated as an imperative here because it fits the context of Paul's argument better. See A. T. Robertson, 4:118. The New American Standard Bible lists this as a possible translation.
20. Arndt and Gingrich, 81.
21. Emil Brunner, *The Christian Doctrine of the Church, Faith, and the Consummation* (Philadelphia: Westminister Press, 1960), 43.
22. Arndt and Gingrich, 413.
23. Strauch, 95.
24. Brunner, 44.

25. Peter Wagner, *Leading Your Church to Growth* (Ventura, Calif.: Regal Books, 1984), 141–65.

26. Ibid., 159.

27. Robert D. Dale, *Pastoral Leadership* (Nashville: Abingdon Press: 1986), 42.

28. Glen Martin and Gary McIntosh, *The Issachar Factor* (Nashville: Broadman & Holman Publishers, 1993), 61.

29. Ibid.

30. Norman Sawchuck, *How to Be a More Effective Church Leader* (Leith, N.Dak.: Spiritual Growth Resources, 1981), 19–20.

31. See G. A. Pritchard, *Willow Creek Seeker Services; Evaluating a New Way of Doing Church* (Grand Rapids: Baker Books 1996) for a discussion of some of the issues.

32. W. Dale Robertson, "The Role of Servant Leadership in Church Growth," D. Min. project, Southeastern Baptist Theological Seminary, 1999, 29ff.

Chapter 6, The Relationship of the Pastor-Elder and the Deacon

1. Thayer, 138.

2. See also Matthew 23:11; Mark 10:43; 9:35.

3. Edward Schweizer, *Church Order in the New Testament* (Napierville, Ill.: Alec R. Allenson, Inc., 1961), 173–74.

4. Moulton and Milligan, 149.

5. Schweizer, 179.

6. Saucy, 154.

7. Arndt and Gingrich, 494.

8. C. K. Barrett, *A Critical and Exegetical Commentary on the Acts of the Apostles,* 2 vols. (Edinburg: T. & T. Clark, 1994), 1:312–13.

9. David John Williams, *Acts* (San Francisco: Harper & Row Publishers, 1985), 103–104.

10. Lea and Griffin, 116.

11. Hendrickson, 131.

12. See comments on 1 Timothy 3:3 on the mixing of wine with water.

13. Kent, 133.

14. Arndt and Gingrich, 24.

15. Charles R. Erdman, *The Pastoral Epistles of Paul* (Philadelphia: Westminister Press, 1928), 43.

16. Lea and Griffin, 117.

17. Kelly, 82.

18. Ibid.

19. Kent, 135.

20. See Hultgren, 75.

21. Ibid.

22. Fairbairn, 150–51.

23. Ibid., 151.

24. See Kelly, 84.

25. Arndt and Gingrich, 670.

26. See Kelly for discussion against the traditional view, 80–81.

27. Barclay, 97–98.

28. Lea and Griffin, 116.

29. Eugene Carson Blake, ed., *Presbyterian Law for the Local Church,* 4th ed. (Philadelphia: Board of Education of the Presbyterian Church in the USA, 1957), 53.

30. Strauch, 30.

Appendix 1: Ecclesiology in the Free Church of the Reformation (1525–1608)

1. William R. Estep, *The Anabaptist Story,* 3d ed. (Grand Rapids: Eerdmans, 1996), 13–14.

2. For more information, see Leonard Verduin, *The Reformers and Their Stepchildren* (Sarasota, Fla.: Christian Hymnary Publishers, 1963).

3. "Elder," *Mennonite Encyclopedia,* 178.

4. Ibid.

5. Balthasar Hubmaier, "A Form for Water Baptism," in H. Wayne Pipkin and John H. Yoder, *Balthasar Hubmaier, Theologian to the Anabaptists* (Scottdale, Pa.: Herald Press, 1989), 388–89.

6. Balthasar Hubmaier, "On the Christian Baptism of Believers," in Pipkin and Yoder, 127.

7. John H. Yoder, trans. and ed., *The Schleitheim Confession* (Scottdale, Pa.: Herald Press, 1977), 13.

8. Ibid., 11.

9. Ibid., 13.

10. Ibid., 13–14.

11. Estep, 165.

12. Menno Simons, "Foundation of Christian Doctrine," in Leonard Verduin, trans. and J. C. Wenger, ed., *The Complete Writings of Menno Simons* (Scottdale, Pa.: Herald Press, 1956), 161.

13. Ibid., 162.

14. Ibid., 163.

15. John Christian Wenger, *Glimpses of Mennonite History and Doctrine* (Scottdale, Pa.: Herald Press, 1992), 144.

16. Ironically, over time the Mennonite denominations in America have evolved into an amalgamation of congregational rule with authority given to district conferences. Cornelius Dyck, one of the most respected Mennonite historians, wrote in his *Introduction to Mennonite History,* "The bishops or pastors, assisted by the deacons or elders, attempt to carry out these standards in the congregation of their charge. Major matters of policy are, however, subject to congregational discussion and decision. . . . Some conferences put more weight on the authority of the bishops and on the decisions of the conference; others are more inclined to stress congregational government" (220).

17. Menno Simons, "The New Birth," in Verduin and Wenger, 94.

18. "Elder," *Mennonite Encyclopedia.*

19. "The Waterlander Confession of Faith," in William L. Lumpkin, *Baptist Confessions of Faith* (Philadelphia: Judson Press, 1959), 58.

20. Ibid., 59.

21. C. Arnold Snyder, *Anabaptist History and Theology,* rev. ed. (Kitchener, Ont.: Pandora Press, 1997), 369.

Appendix 2: Ecclesiology Among Baptists in Great Britain and America
(1609–Present)

1. William L. Lumpkin, *Baptist Confessions of Faith* (Philadelphia: Judson Press, 1959).

2. There were definitely Anabaptists within several of the Separatist congregations of late Elizabethan and early Stuart England, and several of those churches divided over the desire of a portion of the membership to adopt so-called Anabaptist practices. Sometimes this arose from Anabaptist members or contacts with Anabaptists; more often it arose from study of the New Testament. However, we have no clear evidence of an English-speaking Baptist church prior to the Smyth-Helwys congregation's adoption of Baptist views in 1609, only instances of individuals holding one or more of what would become known as Baptist beliefs within Separatist congregations.

3. Lumpkin, 99.

4. Ibid., 101.

5. Ibid.

6. Ibid., 116–23. I have modernized the spellings but nothing else.

7. Ibid., 121–22.

8. Ibid.

9. Ainsworth had been chosen teacher in the Ancient Church, an English Separatist congregation, the majority of which was exiled in Holland because the pastor, Francis Johnson, was still imprisoned in England. Ainsworth rejected the Presbyterian polity of Johnson. Ministers were elected and dismissed by the congregation. The congregation likewise made decisions about membership and church discipline. Ainsworth's "A True Confession" is a landmark in the development of congregational polity. Williston Walker, *The Creeds and Platforms of Congregationalism* (New York: Charles Scribner's Sons, 1893), 59–74.

10. There is no doctrine of reprobation, and the responsibility to preach the gospel to all is included.

11. Lumpkin, 165.

12. Ibid., 166.

13. Ibid., 168.

14. Ibid., 229–30.

15. Ibid., 230–31.

16. By American Baptists, I refer to all Baptists located geographically in America, not just those who are members of the American Baptist Churches in the U.S.A. or its predecessor entities.

17. It was published as the 6th edition. It had been used earlier, at least as early as 1724, but there is no record in the associational minutes of its being formally adopted prior to 1742.

18. Timothy and Denise George, eds., *Baptist Confessions, Covenants, and Catechisms* (Nashville: Broadman and Holman, 1996), 86.

19. Ibid., 134.

20. Lumpkin, 395.

21. George and George, 142.

22. David T. Morgan, *The New Crusades, The New Holy Land: Conflict in the Southern Baptist Convention, 1969–1991* (Tuscaloosa: University of Alabama Press, 1996), 23–24. The proposed constitutional amendment received a majority but not the required two-thirds support.